Views from the Manse

The Author, Rev Peter MacGregor, with his surviving family of 3 children (Margaret (Meta), David and Ian), taken at Kirkhill in 1907.

Views from the Manse

Essays from the pen of a Highland Parish Minister

BY
THE REVEREND PETER MACGREGOR
(1865–1935)

EDITED BY
COLIN FRY

The Pentland Press
Edinburgh – Cambridge – Durham – USA

© C. S. Fry, 1999

First published in 1999 by
The Pentland Press Ltd
1 Hutton Close
South Church
Bishop Auckland
Durham

ISBN 1–85821-668-0

Typeset in Goudy 11/13
by Carnegie Publishing, Carnegie House, Chatsworth Road, Lancaster, LA1 4SL
Printed and bound by Bookcraft Ltd, Bath

*The Editor wishes to dedicate this book
to the memory of his Mother,
Margaret Una Cameron Fry,
daughter of Peter MacGregor,
and to her brothers, David and Ian.*

*Like the Falls in the Glens,
their love of the Highlands,
its people and its Faith, tumbles over
down the generations
even as they travel the world.*

Contents

Illustrations

Foreword

by Sir James Grant of Grant, 33rd Chief of Clan Grant

In nineteenth and early twentieth-century Scotland the minister was both divine and didact – a source of spiritual guidance and of learning. The Reverend Peter MacGregor, a Highlander, was a minister of the Presbyterian Church of Scotland from 1890 to 1935. Passionately interested in the Highlands during the 150 years before his own times, he frequently used his discourses – which were often delivered in Gaelic – to familiarise his parishioners with the history of their own land and people. Now his grandson has collected some of those talks, which paint a vivid history of various aspects of Highland life over almost two centuries.

Writing on topics as diverse as the devastating consequences of Culloden; the minutiae of daily existence on a Strathspey farm in the 1770s; that unique fount of 'mad wisdom', 'The Highland Fool'; and the life and ministry of Saint Columba, MacGregor draws on a wide range of sources, both historical and anecdotal, to provide concise and accessible vignettes.

For the last twenty-three years of his life, MacGregor was the minister at Duthil, at the very church which is now the headquarters of the Clan Grant Society, which gives his work an added interest for members of my clan. Having lived all my adult life on the right side of the Highland Line and having farmed in the region, I found his talks of particular personal interest.

I can heartily recommend *Views from the Manse* to anyone wishing to discover more about Highland history.

Map of Scotland showing the 100 km squares of the National Grid and principle towns and districts mentioned in the book. Approximate position of each of the places listed in the Places Index can be found by reference to their Ordnance Survey grid letter and number (the first two digits giving a coordinate east of the gridline; e.g. Kingussie is on the edge of square NH, 75 km east and oo km north from the southwest corner). For more accurate positioning refer to the appropriate OS Landranger series map given in the Index. (Map redrawn after *Atlas of the World* Geo Philip & Son Ltd. 1980) © Crown Copyright

Introduction

As an all too distant observer of life in that most ruggedly beautiful land that makes up the Highlands of Scotland and its people, it seems to me that the viewpoint of a minister of the Kirk, at least up to the early days of the twentieth century, was in some ways unique. He not only officiated at the deepest moments in the lives of each of his parishioners, sharing the joy of their fulfilments and the agony of their failures, he also fulfilled a sensory role in discerning the changing nature of the Highland community, and a more active part in seeking to promote its vitality and cohesion. He was himself part of its fierce independence, yet committed himself to building its parochial life as a microcosm of the Kingdom of Heaven.

Peter MacGregor was a minister of the presbyterian Church of Scotland from May, 1890 until his sudden death in the Duthil Parish at Carrbridge in December 1935. Born into the farming community at Fearnan, near Kenmore on the shores of Loch Tay, his early life was not cushioned from the uncertainties of land tenure in the mid-nineteenth century – his father John had to vacate his tenancy at Boreland owing to his own father's early death at the age of 48 in 1848.

John, however, had escaped the exodus, finding work as a farm manager on the Earl of Breadalbane's estate at Taymouth Castle and Peter was thus educated first in the village school at Acharn; the same school, incidentally, to which his kinsman Rob Roy MacGregor had entrusted his sons, when hounded from Glengyle some 150 years before. Peter showed such diligence and aptitude here that he progressed to Raining's School, Inverness (see Appendix 1) and eventually, as one of Dr MacBain's brightest pupils, to Edinburgh University, where he won a number of bursaries and medals, including the Jeffery Scholarship in Church History. He remained, nevertheless, a Highlander with his heart in the hills; fluent in Gaelic and fascinated by the changes which had taken place over the 150 years or so before his own ministry began.

Licensed in Kintyre on the 16th May, 1890, Peter committed himself to a ministry of evangelical and social involvement in the lives of his various parishes. He first served as Assistant to the Revd Peter Mac - Kenzie (Moderator of the Church of Scotland from 1884) at Ferintosh on the Black Isle, before being given his own charge of Ballachulish and Glencoe in January, 1891. In the Spring of 1896 he moved some 180 miles north to Lochinver and the Parish of Assynt, to which he took his newly-wed, Maggie, a month later. Two years later he was back south, this time on the Isle of Mull at Tobermory, where his four children were born: Helen (1896), Margaret (usually known as Meta) (1901), David (1904) and Ian (1906). Sadly, Helen died of diphtheria two weeks after her seventh birthday. The move to Kirkhill (home of the Lovat Frasers) in September, 1907 was followed by further tragedy four and a half months later when Maggie also died, leaving the Minister to bring up the remaining three children with the help and constant compan - ionship of his cousin Margaret (also Maggie) MacDonald.

From these scattered Highland parishes and from a wide range of historical sources, Peter must have spent many of his solitary hours in these remote hillsides gathering the information for this collage of Highland life. Possibly only in his later years at Kirkhill and after 1912 at Duthil, were his views written into a series of exercise books, and presented as talks to his parishioners as a means of education, enlight - enment and entertainment before the days of radio and television. They thus formed part of an effective and much appreciated ministry to the social, educational and spiritual welfare of his people.

He was described by one colleague as a silent man, yet it was the silence of a man who had trained himself to listen and to think well before he spoke. When the opportunity came, in 1930, of uniting the established church at Duthil with the United Free Church at nearby Carrbridge, he was as readily accepted by the wider church, having already won their affection by his lack of denominational bias and his common interest in the people and their needs. He was chairman of the local amenities association, the public institute and sports clubs as well as serving on the education authority and as chairman of the Badenoch school management committee.

Although much of the information given may be accessible elsewhere to the serious student of Scottish social history, I believe Peter's per - spective and first-hand experience of life in the Highlands and Islands,

The Manse, Tobermory in 1906, with the family of the Author, including (left to right): daughter Helen Kinloch (7), wife Margaret (Maggie) Watson, Mrs Helen Hodge (wife's mother) holding son David Patrick (2), the author, second daughter Margaret Una Cameron (Meta) (5) and maid Mary.

together with his interpretation for 'the common man', make this a most valuable and overdue contribution to Scottish literature. It has taken over a century in the making. I hope you will find it worth waiting for.

Each chapter is a distinct topic in itself and can be read in total isolation from the others. Together, however, they paint a picture of life in the eighteenth and early nineteenth centuries in all its interactions, its social system, its economic and political isolation and its religious and cultural heritage. The first three essays are pure social history. They are followed by two biographical chapters. The first follows one of the most colourful Highland characters of the Jacobean period – Simon, Lord Lovat of Beauly, the last person to be beheaded at the Tower of London. The book is then rounded off with a view of St Columba, the 1400th anniversary of whose death in Iona was remembered in 1997.

One chapter in particular (The Highland Fool) makes use of the author's familiarity with the Gaelic language (in which I am told he preached his best sermons) – translations are included – as well as local dialect. I am deeply indebted to William MacDonald, Headmaster of Liniclate School, Benbecula for assisting in the transcription of the Gaelic sections. Where William gave me alternatives to the original, I tried to make a choice based on keeping as close to my grandfather's rendering as was possible, consistent with modern Gaelic practice. I therefore accept full responsibility for any errors and should be glad to receive notification of them.

As editor, I freely acknowledge my own unfamiliarity, not only with the language but to some extent with places and customs. Margaret, Peter's daughter and my mother, married a 'Sasannach' three years before Peter's death and spent the remainder of her life in far off Dorset, though with frequent visits to the land she loved until her death in June, 1995. In my research towards this publication, however, I have tried to ensure the accuracy of places and people, for which my grandfather would have strived. I hope I have found most, at least, of his original sources and, together with my own more recent references and other information I thought might be of interest to the modern reader, have acknowledged them in a series of footnotes as well as in the Bibliography. I have also included, in the Places Index, Ordnance Survey references to each of the places mentioned. These are mainly for the infrequent visitor, like myself, who wishes to bring a historical focus to his travels. I am grateful to Ordnance Survey, Shepheard-Walwyn Ltd, National Trust for Scotland and House of Lochar for use of their copyright material and apologise to any others whose material I may inadvertently have used without such permission.

I gratefully record the help and encouragement given by my publishers; by Inverness Archivist, Bob Steward; Miss Fiona MacLeod and Miss Edwina Burridge of the Inverness Reference Library; Mrs Rachel Chisholm and staff at the Highland Folk Museum at Kingussie; Mr Coghill of Ardliosta (Lovat historian) and the Property Manager of Saltram House (National Trust), Plympton for use of the Earl of Morley's collection of Thomas Pennant's *Tour of Scotland*. For filling gaps in my knowledge of the author's life I wish to thank Louise McCarron of the National Library of Scotland and my sister Ruth Knight, who remembered to ask the right questions at the right time to produce an extensive family tree. Finally my appreciation must go to my wife and family for their patience and help during the hours of typing and checking, and to my father for presenting me with the challenge of bringing these essays to life again after so many years.

They are presented here, in book form, in the hope of providing both those with their roots in the hills and those who simply appreciate the unique character of the Highlands, with a readable, historical review of some of the most formative generations of life in this beautiful region of Scotland.

CSF

Note
Maps are based on the Ordnance Survey map with the permission of the Controller of Her Majesty's Stationery Office, ©Crown Copyright MC 88761M0001

Chapter 1

The Highlands After Culloden

In the history of the Highlands there is no landmark which can be compared to the '45. The wants of that year were the means directly and indirectly of effecting great change and particularly of breaking down the rampart that tended to separate the Highlands from the rest of Scotland. Marked distinctions still remained and remain to this day, for however you may assimilate laws, past traditions and racial charac-teristics cannot be eradicated with the same ease that you can alter the dress or change the legal system of a people. Nevertheless, it was a momentous change which resulted from the disastrous result of Prince Charles's gallant venture to regain the throne of his fathers.

Hitherto the southern parts of Britain knew very little of the High-lands, of the true character and condition of those who dwelt within those mountain fortresses. They did, indeed, see rough, uncouth-looking individuals, clad in strange garb, driving herds of black cattle south along the cattle tracks that led to the great fairs, but they seldom tried to converse with them. They were moved by little curiosity to know what the country was like from which they came. If they thought of it at all, they imagined it to be a grim repulsive inclement land without beauty or attractiveness, a land of black bleak moors and sterile frowning mountains, a land to be avoided by all who could. It is true that means of communication between Highland and Lowland had been much improved before Culloden. The military roads which had been con-structed from 1725 onwards under the direction of General Wade and Major William Caulfeild, and which came to be of incalculable service to the country afterwards, enabled those who wished to penetrate with comparative ease into the very heart of the Highlands. But few did use them except those constrained by duty to do so or Highland chiefs on their way to enjoy the pleasures of the Capitals of England or Scotland.

Dr Johnson says somewhere that people in South Britain were almost as ignorant of the Highlands as they were of Borneo. Till after the '45 it was regarded as a wild country of warring clans, of formidable barbarians who knew nothing and cared for nothing except to split heads and drink quaichs (goblets) of strong drink; a people of alien language, manners and dress, without culture of any kind, robbing what they could, fighting whenever they had an excuse. The country had evidently almost no resources to attract the adventurous and enterprising. The people were poor, their wants were few because they had little with which to buy. Blood or ancestry alone gave dignity, not wealth in money.

At that time, the modern admiration for natural scenery was as yet little felt. The rugged grandeur of our Highlands did not appeal then as it does today. 'An eye accustomed to flowering pastures and waving harvests,' said Dr Johnson in describing his visit to Scotland in 1773, 'is astonished and repelled by this wide extent of hopeless sterility.'[1] It seemed so easy sitting at home to conceive a barren image of rocks and heath and waterfalls that it might seem a journey into this ragged mountain land would be useless labour, which would neither excite the imagination nor enlarge the understanding. We ascribe this modern love of nature to such poets as Burns and Wordsworth and to Sir Walter Scott, but I think we owe more of it than has yet been recognised to our Highland (Gaelic) poets themselves. But speaking generally of the period before the '45, we can say that the Highlands were to a large extent an unknown land, repelling rather than attracting, feared rather than admired.

After the '45 a great change took place, both in the condition of things within the Highland pale and in the attitude of the southern people. So completely was the rebellion crushed and so rigorously and effectively was the Disarming Act of 1748 carried out that the old terror of the Highland-ers soon died away. This Act forbade not only the carrying of arms but the wearing of distinctive Highland dress. Any of you familiar with Gaelic poetry may remember the universal lament of the poets of that age over this, their diatribes against cramping trews and black surtouts so different from lightsome bonnet, plaid and philabeg.[2]

The gallantry of the Highlanders in that rising was indeed recognised

---

1   Dr Samuel Johnson *Journey to the Western Islands*, 1785.
2   The kilt, from Gaelic *feileadh beag*, literally 'a little fold or wrap'. For a full discussion of the origins and variations of Highland dress see Micheil MacDonald *The Clans of Scotland*, 1991 pp. 34–48.

throughout Scotland. Jacobitism, now that it had ceased to be an active menace, became a romantic sentiment and the land where Prince Charles had found such loyalty and devotion began to exercise a certain fascination. It is a common experience to find that what has been an object of terror, once its power is broken, becomes an object of attraction. The Highlands, hitherto the home of wild terrifying warriors, became now the sanctuary of romance.

With the Disarming Act, other measures were taken to remove the differences between the Highlands and the rest of the country. The clan system was broken, the hereditary jurisdiction of the great chiefs was taken from them, and the people became subject to the system of civil law and government as it prevailed through the remainder of Britain. Hitherto, these great chiefs like Lovat, Seaforth and others had the right of making out justice within the bounds of their own lands; they had in legal terminology the power of 'sock, sack, pit and gallows'; they acted as Sheriffs or Lord Justices, held their courts and punished crimes.

In those times under that system and considering the inaccessibility of the glens and islands, probably nothing better could have been devised than what was by its nature a rough system of justice. For I imagine the chiefs of those times were fitter for a battlefield than the judicial bench, having had little training in that calm, equable, impartial temper of mind we look for in our judges. The consequence was that justice was often administered with vindictive severity and the moot hills became simply gallows hills (*Tom na Croiche*).[3]

In my native parish I was well acquainted with the place where the Campbells of Breadalbane sat to administer justice and whenever a MacGregor fell into their hands justice very promptly decided his fate without the need of too many witnesses. History tells how James Stewart of the Glens was indicted for the murder of Campbell of Glenure – and that after the '45 – and how the Duke of Argyll presided at the trial and fourteen Campbells sat on the jury.[4] Could the judicial result in

---

3   e.g. Gallows Knoll near Kenmore, close to the Author's birthplace – cited by A. Macgregor Hutcheson in an article *An Coille Dhubh* in the Clan Gregor Soc. newsletter Spring 1997, p. 21.

4   See also the trial of Alistair, Chief of Macgregor in Edinburgh in 1604, after the Glen Fruin massacre of 1603, where the jury was picked from men of Dumbarton and Argyll. According to the account in *Clan Gregor* by Forbes MacGregor (1977)

such a case lie for a moment in doubt, however weak the evidence of guilt might be? Although the forms of legality might be kept, it was scarcely to be expected that a jury of vassals would decide in any other way than as they knew their superior desired. They were too dependent to be relied on to act according to the dictates of strict justice.

This jurisdiction also kept the clansmen under the hand of their chief, practically constrained to do whatever he wished, to minister to his wants in peace and to rise with him in war. The new Act secured to them a liberty hitherto unknown; they were not bound to him as they had been; they could go where they pleased without let or hindrance. A spirit of adventure and independence began to spring up among them.

Before the '45, Highlanders began to be enrolled in the army, at first ostensibly for the purpose of guarding the Highland Line and protecting the lowlanders from raids. It was for this purpose the Black Watch was raised. Soon, however, an excuse was found for sending them abroad where they fought with redoubtable valour in Flanders, particularly at Fontenoy, [5] winning the admiration of their commander. After the suppression of the Jacobite rising, an impetus was given to this recruiting for the King's service and especially when the French War broke in 1756. Pitt, with the eagle eye of genius, saw an opportunity of utilising the dormant military spirit of the Highlanders by giving commissions to their chiefs in the British Army in new regiments to be raised among the clans.

The project was wonderfully successful. The warlike spirit revived, the regiments were permitted to wear the Highland dress, otherwise forbidden, and they went forth to shed their blood on many a hard-fought field, winning for their country and themselves immortal renown. For example, the Fraser Highlanders, under the son of Simon, Lord Lovat, were the first to scale the Heights of Abraham and foremost in the battle line which won Quebec and Canada for Britain. Those who survived that great war, which ended in 1763, came back from Canada to tell of that vast country where they had fought, with momentous

---

cont. it was the commission given by James VI to the Colquhouns, supported by Argyll and the townsfolk of Dumbarton, which initiated the affair. But the Court was not interested in justice, only revenge.

5   Battle of Fontenoy 1745. Like Culloden a year later, the British forces were led by the Duke of Cumberland. Unlike Culloden, they were heavily defeated by the French, the allies losing half of their 50,000 men.

consequences for their countrymen. A larger world than his own narrow glens and sea-girt isles loomed before the restless mind of the Highlander and that movement began, which has carried and is still carrying the offspring of the narrow mountain land away to the vast West.

Another influence in the changes taking place, and rapidly acceler-ating then, was the publication of the Poems of Ossian in English in 1760.[6] The vexed question of the authenticity of these poems is not to be discussed here. On their appearance, they certainly startled and astonished the literary world of the day. Coming from an unknown land, from a people believed to be absolutely devoid of all culture or aesthetic sensibility, whose language was supposed to have no written documents and no literary memorials, these poems naturally caused a great storm of excitement and controversy. On the one side was a band of writers, mostly Scots, who maintained their genuineness, and lauded their beauty in language that sounds strange to us today. These Scottish writers were really not very capable of deciding the value of proofs offered, any more than the opponents of MacPherson were of disproving the genuineness of the poems, but they wrote as if their national glory was at stake.

Dr Blair wrote a dissertation, not only defending their authenticity, but also ranking them with the poems of Homer and Virgil. The age was commonplace enough and perhaps sensible of its unheroic character. Therefore it was more susceptible to the mysterious, the romantic and sentimental, ready to welcome some new appeal to its imagination. Ossian came opportunely, it touched certain chords of feeling and imagination which vibrated responsively to it, gave glimpses of unfamil-iar scenes seen through the golden haze of years, and helped to initiate a new romanticism which was to affect literature, politics and even religion. It is scarcely possible for us to understand the furore over these poems, the delight with which they were read. Young ladies filled their letters with quotations from them and generals carried them to the field of battle.

The great protagonist against their authenticity was Dr Samuel

---

6   James MacPherson *Fragments of Ancient Poetry*, 1760. There is considerable doubt over the authenticity of these translations of Ossianic ballads by the one-time Schoolmaster of Kingussie; but there is ample evidence for a distinct Scottish Gaelic literary tradition from such authors as Sir James MacGregor, *The Book of the Dean of Lismore*, 1512–26.

Johnson. Prejudiced against anything Scots – although, strange to say, his reputation today depends, not on his Dictionary, but on a Scotsman, James Boswell – so time takes its revenges. Dr Johnson naturally assumed an antagonistic attitude. Yet he was interested in the Highlands, for his father had put Martin's account of the Hebrides in his hand when a lad and from that day he had been anxious to visit the country and its people. This Ossianic controversy whetted his interest and more than once he spoke to Boswell of taking a journey to the Highlands. He wished to see that patriarchal system of clanship ere it had entirely passed away. Also, feeling convinced that the Poems of Ossian had never existed save in MacPherson's brain, he wished to prove his case by personal enquiry on the spot. Meeting also with some of the Hebridean chiefs like Sir James MacDonald, that remarkable Admiral Crichton of the Hebrides, he had been very favourably impressed by them and wished to visit them in their own homes.

After delaying from year to year, he at last in August 1773, an old man of 63, set out upon his remarkable journey. He arrived in Edinburgh and, travelling with Mr Boswell from thence by Aberdeen and the coast road, arrived at Inverness on Saturday 28th August. Procuring horses there, they proceeded to penetrate the recesses of the Highlands. Surely not since Don Quixote and Sancho Panza set out on their knight errantry did such a pair of equestrians present themselves to view as those two. Very unlike the lanky Spanish gentleman was the ponderous figure of Dr Johnson. His person was large, robust, approaching to the gigantic and grown unwieldy from corpulency. His face was large and disfigured with scrofule; his sight was weak, his mouth often moving with convulsive twitches and from frequent muttering to himself. He wore a wide brown greatcoat with huge pockets and he carried in his hand a large oak stick. Such was the likeness of that most notable figure to whom we owe an admirable account of the condition of things in the more remote Highlands and particularly in the Islands during the generation after Culloden.[7]

Leaving Inverness these two proceeded by the military road to Fort Augustus, from where they rode westward by Glenmoriston and Glenshiel to Glenelg; crossed over from there to Armadale in Skye, thence

---

7   Johnson 1785; also Boswell, A *Tour to the Hebrides with Samuel Johnson*, 1785.

Map of Scotland showing Military Roads constructed 1725 to 1800 from Wm Taylor, *The Military Roads in Scotland*, 1996 (by kind permission). Map also indicates route taken by Mr Boswell and Dr Johnson on their Tour through Scotland and the Hebrides in 1773.

Key:

— Military Roads
······ Dr Johnson's Tour

© Crown Copyright

to Broadford and Corry, from where they crossed to Raasay. Recrossing to Portree, they next visited Kingsburgh, the mistress of which at the time was the renowned Flora MacDonald. From Dunvegan they travelled back to Armadale and got a smack there which carried them to Coll. Having sailed from there to Tobermory, they crossed Mull to Ulva, Inch Kenneth and Iona, then back to Lochbuie. Crossing to Oban, they journeyed by Loch Awe to Inveraray and thence to Loch Lomond and Glasgow – a long and trying journey for an old man unaccustomed to rough roads and rougher seas.

Although Dr Johnson was the most notable visitor of that time, he was preceded and succeeded by several others who have given us accounts of their experiences. For example, an Irish Bishop, Dr Pococke, visited the Highlands in 1760, travelling north through Argyllshire, along the Great Glen and then north to Sutherland and Caithness. A Scottish Bishop, Dr Forbes has left us an account of his visitation of the episco-palian communities in Ross, Inverness and Argyll about 1770. But a more valuable account than either of these was that of an English naturalist, Thomas Pennant, who paid two visits to the North in 1769 and 1772.[8] On the first occasion he passed through the Highlands of Perthshire and Aberdeenshire, north along the coast of Caithness, then back to Inverness and from there by the military road to Fort William, Tyndrum and Inveraray. On the second occasion he also visited the Islands of Arran, Islay, Iona, Rhum and Skye and the western seaboard of Rossshire and Invernessshire.

Accounts like these stimulated the curiosity of others and from that date the stream of visitors gradually increased to the present day when we watch it hurrying past by car and by rail. Dr Johnson confessed that he had come a generation too late to see what he expected: 'a system of antiquated life'. Many traces of the old system, of the old relationship between chiefs and people, still remained at that date but they were rapidly passing away. Everything was being assimilated to the customs prevailing in the South. The chiefs, small and great, began to find their way southward, many of them to London – not always either to their own advantage or that of their people. One with a rent-roll of £500

---

8   Thomas Pennant: *A Tour in Scotland & Voyage to the Hebrides* (3 vols) 5th edition, 1790.

and the pride of a noble ancestry was tempted to measure his expenditure in accordance with the name he bore, rather than with the money in his purse.

Moreover, lavish hospitality had been the habit of these men. The old bards who were retainers of the chiefs delighted to laud their munificent generosity, the superabundance of food and drink that loaded their tables. There were almost no houses of entertainment in the country for travellers because there was no need for them. It was a point of honour to entertain travellers and so every gentleman's house became a place of entertainment. This custom of almost prodigal hospitality continued even into the nineteenth century. I remember an old farmer telling me how they used, on their return from Falkirk Tryst, to travel from farmhouse to farmhouse, being entertained in princely style. This was a survival of the customs of a former age where every chief kept open house and every tacksman followed his example. There was a welcome for every traveller, nothing was grudged and I fear there was little economy. The chief was surrounded by a crowd of needy retainers and dependants, who hung about his castle doing little.

Mrs Grant of Laggan gives a vivid description of the scene at Simon, Lord Lovat's table; how at the top part would be placed the noble friends he liked to have about him, further down would be smaller cadets of the Lovat family whom he designated as cousins, and further down the hall the poorer class of retainers. And the class of food placed before these guests varied according to their social station, from French wines to tuppenny ale, from venison to sheep's head.[9] That, on a large scale, represents the scene in many a chief's house up till about the '45 but seldom, I think, after it.

New ideas entered then, the relationship between chief and people altered, the chiefs became lairds or owners of property, not heads of clans. An old gentleman related to Dr Johnson that, forty years before, a chieftain walked out attended by ten or twelve followers with their arms rattling. That retinue had now been done away with and gradually an estrangement grew between the chief and the people under him. He regarded them and they regarded him in a different manner from what they had been accustomed to do. In former days, a MacDonald or

---

9   See Ch 4, p. 105.

Macleod was esteemed according to the number of his followers, the number he could muster under his standard to fight, and even the number that would accompany him to a funeral. Now these were of little account to determine his station in society. The commercial spirit had displaced the martial; a new criterion was the standard of a man's eminence. He was held in reputation not according to the size of his property or the number of inhabitants on it, but according to the amount of his income. One chief, on being asked as to the rent of his estate, replied that it could raise five hundred men. But now that the clans were disarmed and the hereditary jurisdiction taken away, the number of men was of little account.

The proprietors of these highland estates, as we may now term them, found when they went south that the rents charged by them were much beneath those charged for lands of equal extent there and also that the number of people was excessive for the productivity of the land. The temptation, in former days, was to divide and subdivide the land in order to increase the number under the chief's standard and undoubtedly, in the conditions that subsisted, the population on these poor patches of ill-cultured land was excessive. From 1760 onward the temptation was altogether in the opposite direction. Expenses in one direction were diminished by dismissing superfluous dependants and reducing the staff of half-idle servants kept. Then rents began to be raised, strangers began to enter into competition for land with those who had held hereditary possession for ages and, offering higher rent, displaced the former occu-piers.

A word must be said on the mode of tenure prevailing then throughout the Highlands, particularly the Western Highlands and Islands. The land was held under the chief or proprietor by tacksmen who were themselves often of the family of the chief, at least gentlemen in the Highland sense of that word. These did not so much work the land themselves as farm it out to subtenants in what we would call crofting communities. Not only did these subtenants pay rent to the tacksmen, they had at the same time to submit to various exactions such as tilling and sowing his land, gathering the harvest, providing peats for his house, thatching part of his steading. Lower in the social grade than these were the scalys or cottars who had to render various services with almost no remuneration except grass for a cow and an occasional peck of meal.

The tacksmen were probably the first to feel the adverse effects of the new conditions by having the rent of their land doubled and trebled.

The innkeeper at Aonach[10] in Glenmoriston told Dr Johnson that the rent of his farm which, twenty years before, had been £5, was now raised to £20 and he could not make a living out of it. On the MacDonald Estates Sir Alexander had displaced more than one of the former tacksmen by letting their land to strangers at greatly increased rents. But speedily the bulk of the people felt the effect of this policy; their crofts also had their rents increased, while the larger farmers required fewer servants. No doubt more had been kept than were really required, a tacksman paying £50 per year keeping as many as twenty servants, many of them doubtless hereditary dependants on the family.

For the surplus population and in relief of this strain, an outlet appeared in emigration. After the end of the French War, in 1763, the tide of emigration set in very strongly, among the first to go being many of the tacksmen. These had constituted the officers of the Highland regiments and having seen the wide expanses of the New World, waiting to be occupied, many of them settled there in place of returning home, while they sent glowing accounts of their new homes back to their native land. I believe you will find on the banks of the St Lawrence the descendants of MacDonalds and Frasers who intermarried with the French and now talk little but French themselves.[11] Their friends caught the contagion and numbers followed, the tacksmen from a motive of independence, the poor from attachment to them and with the hope of bettering their condition. Kingsburgh, for example, the husband of Flora MacDonald, emigrated to America shortly after Dr Johnson was there, although some years afterwards he returned.

The Highland proprietors did not view this emigration with favour because it drew away the wealthier and more capable among their tenants; little however was done to check it. From 1770 onward it became a very rage and from all parts of the Highlands they hived away to the West, some to Carolina, some to Connecticut, many to Nova

---

10   Wm Taylor in *The Military Roads in Scotland*, 1996 (p. 156), states that although Johnson claimed the inn was 9 miles from Fort Augustus, which places it near Ceannacroc Bridge, there is now no trace of it.

11   For families like the Frasers this was a return to even earlier roots, re-establishing their Norman connection; see Ch 4 p. 94.

Scotia and Cape Breton. From Skye itself, between 1771–90, eight emigrant ships carried 2,400 souls away. Even from far inland parts many joined the stream passing to the West.

Of course, this tide of emigration was strongest where the people were most discontented and dejected. In some parts the proprietors set them-selves to check emigration by endeavouring to make their people contented. For example, Sir James Grant of Grant laboured assiduously to make his people in Urquhart contented and prosperous by introducing new industries and improving their tillage. The Forfeited Estates Com-missioners also, who had among others the Lovat Estates under their charge, did much for the tenantry. They spent their profits in founding schools for instruction in spinning; they gave flax seed to farmers and wheels to poor people. They also expended money in making roads and planting timber.

It is evident from the various accounts we have of the state of the Highlands in the generation after Culloden, that there was much misery and discontent throughout the country. The people were in general wretchedly poor and miserably housed. We sometimes remark upon the number that once inhabited a parish compared to its present population but let us also take into account how they subsisted, how meagre was the provision for keeping body and soul together. Much ignorance still prevails regarding the condition of the people then. It is sometimes assumed that they had abundance to eat and drink and liberties unknown nowadays. But the vivacious testimony of those times does not draw any such roseate picture.

On one island farm – and this is typical – the chief labourer had fifty shillings a year and a stone of meal per week for the support of his family and himself. A principal herdsman had as wages grass for two cows and meal sufficient for his family; a cowherd had twenty-four shillings a year and shoes, and one under him had sixteen shillings. Two others, who acted as ploughmen, had grass for two cows and six sheep, the tenth sheaf and as many potatoes as they chose to plant. House-keepers had £3 a year and the maidservants from £1 to thirty shillings. For ordinary work wages were from threepence to sixpence per day. Skilled labour like mason work got from sixpence to eightpence per day – not per hour as now [1920s]. On such remuneration as that what comforts could be procured? But, says someone, they had plenty of potatoes, meal and milk. As to potatoes they may have had plenty, but only too often both meal and milk were very scarce and when barley or oatmeal had to be bought it cost from ten shillings to fifteen shillings per bale.

Pennant gives a pathetic account of the people in the Western Isles when he visited them in 1772. The year 1771 had been inclement and there had been a partial failure of crops so that the people had to subsist largely on milk and shellfish. Bishop Pococke, writing in 1760 of Sutherlandshire, says: 'The people live very hardy on milk, curds, whey and a little oatmeal. Their best food consists of oat and barley cakes. A porridge of oatmeal, cale and sometimes a piece of salt meat in it is their top fare. They have not yet come to the use of potatoes but a small beginning. In the middle and south of Scotland they are in plenty.' By 1770 however potatoes were rapidly becoming the staple food of the people in the West. They were introduced by MacDonald of Clanranald from Ireland into Uist in 1743 but for a time they were not regarded with favour. Then it was discovered that they could grow almost anywhere and produced a prolific crop. So they soon became the mainstay of their lives. 'Potatoes have now become one of the principal parts of their food,' says Johnson.

If their food was poor, their houses were even more wretched. Captain Burt in his letters from the Highlands[12] mentions that in Inverness the best houses were low roofed, built of rubble stone and harled.[13] The poorer parts of the town were 'made up of miserably low dirty hovels, faced and covered with turf with a bottomless tub or basket in the roof for a chimney.' Thirty years later the ordinary type of house occupied by the common people was no better. They were as bad in the Islands as on the mainland. The typical Island house was constructed of drystone with a roof of turf thatched with heath, held down by withies weighted with heavy stones. It had neither window nor chimney. The fire was placed in the middle of the floor and a hole was made in the roof for the smoke, not directly over the fire lest the rain might extinguish it.

---

12 Capt Edmund Burt *Letters from a Gentleman in the North of Scotland* (2 vols) 1754, reprinted Edinburgh 1974. Burt was, in 1725, appointed Receiver General and Collector of the unsold Forfeited Estates in North Britain.

13 I.e. walls treated with rendering of lime and gravel, similar to pebble-dashing in the south of England.

The smoke found its way out as best it could through that hole or through the open door. In one part of the house would be found cows or goats, while the fowls found a place on the rafters, the ducks under the beds. These houses are not extinct in the Highlands yet, but they are now the exception.

'The houses of the peasants in Lochaber,' says Pennant, 'are the most wretched that can be imagined; framed of upright poles which are wattled; the roof is formed of boughs like a wigwam and the whole is covered over with sods, so that in this moist climate their cottages have a perpetual and finer verdure than the rest of the country.'[14] In Glenurquhart in 1763, Lorimer, tutor to the Laird of Grant, tells us that the tenants lived in turf-roofed houses which were constructed of turf, timber and wicker-work. The Lairds had already prohibited the use of timber for walls – I suppose because it was becoming valuable – and the result was that the people began to build drystone walls four or five feet in height. The houses of the better classes were sometimes not a great improvement on these. Many of the farmers dwelt in these hut-like houses, only they had windows and doors and chimneys, and wooden floors in their best rooms. Yet the chamber in which Dr Johnson slept in the Laird of Ulva's house had only a clay floor and when he undressed he found his feet in wet mire.[15]

I have known strangers to be surprised how decent and respectable looking were the people that issued on Sabbath from these wretched-looking hovels. The same surprise was felt by Pennant when he saw how 'well and neatly clad' were the worshippers in Kenmore Church – 'not a ragged or slovenly person among them.'[16] And however mean their houses, however adverse their circumstances, their character receives uniform commendation from all travellers. They are indeed accused of being indolent, but that was because, so Pennant recognises, they had never been accustomed to steady work, never had the opportunity of doing it, considered much drudgery and mean toil beneath them, so left it to women to do it. In Aberdeenshire, that home of the most industrious section of our British population, he found the men

---

14 Pennant 1790, Vol I, p. 229–30.
15 Boswell 1785, p. 288.
16 Pennant 1790, Vol I, p. 102.

'thin but strong, idle and lazy except employed in the chace, or anything that looks like amusement. The women more industrious, spin their own husbands' cloaths and get money by knitting stockings, the great trade of the country.'[17]

I once heard a friend express surprise to a Lewis minister that the women were permitted to do work which rather belonged to men. 'Ah, but you must remember,' was the reply, 'that the women are much stronger here than the men.' So it may have been felt throughout the Highlands about 1770, for they got a large share of the most toilsome labour. 'The women,' Pennant also remarked, 'are most remarkably plain and soon acquire an old look, and by being much exposed to the weather without hats, such a grin and contraction of muscles as heightens greatly their natural hardness of features.' And he adds: 'but the *ne-plus-ultra* of hard features is not found till you arrive among the fish-women of Aberdeen.'[18]

While animadverting on these defects, travellers express a high opinion of their character. 'The people,' says Bishop Pococke, 'are hospitable, charitable, civil, polite and sensible.' And similarly, Pennant says: 'They are indolent unless roused to war or, I may say from experience, to lend any disinterested assistance to the distressed traveller either in directing him on his way or affording their aid in passing the dangerous torrents of the Highlands; hospitable to the highest degree and full of generosity and have in themselves a natural politeness which often flows from the meanest when le[a]st expected. [They] are excessively inquisitive after your business and when they can procure an old newspaper, will listen to it with all the avidity of Shakespeare's blacksmith. [They] have much pride and consequently are impatient of affronts and revengeful of injuries; [yet] are decent in their general behaviour, inclined to superstition, yet attentive to the duties of religion.'[19] Dr Johnson is very gallant and says of one: 'We knew that the girls of the Highlands are all gentlewomen and treated her with great respect, which she received as what was customary and due.'

Let us look for a moment at their industries and what the resources

---

17 Pennant 1790, Vol I, p. 131.
18 Pennant 1790, Vol I, pp. 131–3.
19 Pennant 1790, Vol I, p. 214–15.

of the country were. The people were for the most part engaged in the tillage of the soil, in herding or in fishing. The cultivation of the soil was poor and the results meagre. In the Western Highlands they had not separate and enclosed farms or fields but generally cultivated a certain portion in common on what was called the run-rig principle. Rotation of crops was almost unknown and all was done in the most haphazard way. A portion of land was possessed in common, yearly divided into lots and cultivated according to his taste by the one whose lot happened upon it. Such communism did not, I fear, make for improvement, for in the imperfect state of human nature it is unlikely that a man would spend much labour on improving what might be another's next year and with which he might deal wastefully.

Land was, in the Islands, manured chiefly by seaweed, sometimes by shell sand and burnt limestone; on the mainland, by whatever cattle manure might be procured and by lime where obtainable. The chief crops consisted of oats, barley and bere, an inferior kind of barley. The return from barley might be six to sevenfold, but from oats it was only three to fourfold, and considering that out of that they had to take seed and food, the profit was practically non-existent for payment of rent. Turnips had been introduced in a few places. The young Laird of Coll had introduced them to that island and had sowed and thinned them with his own hands. About Beauly wheat and turnips were planted and produced good crops. A considerable proportion of the barley ingathered was used for the distillation of whisky, private stills being quite common.

One crop which was very extensively grown at that time but is nowhere cultivated now, is flax for linen. I have often heard old people tell of the labours connected with its culture. The use of cotton practically ruined this industry. At that period flax was grown throughout Scotland and the Highlands in Perthshire, Argyllshire and Invernessshire. For example, in Breadalbane much flax was grown in 1770, as much as £2,000 worth of yarn being sold out of the country a few years previously. In the Inverness district it was also cultivated under the fostering care of the Forfeited Estates Commissioners, and in Glenmoriston we find about the year 1760 a linen factory maintained out of the proceeds of the Forfeited Estates, which gave employment to a number of people, including forty women. It is possible that some of you have in your houses linen spun by grandmothers and great-grand-mothers, as I have.

Another industry which has now practically disappeared, but was very active at this period – and active where it was most needed in the islands – was the manufacture of Kelp. It was discovered that carbonate of soda, which was largely used in the making of soap and glass, could be extracted from the ashes of burnt seaweed, and at once a source of revenue appeared where it was least expected. Barren rocks became valuable and infertile islands became prosperous. We first hear of Kelp in Tiree in the year 1746 and from this time the making of it increased rapidly. In 1768 the produce of the western coast of Scotland exceeded 5,000 tons at a price of £6 10s. per ton.

In one way this precarious industry became disastrous in its effect. It attracted people to these barren rocky shores, the population increased there by leaps and bounds so that when, after the great French War, the Kelp industry fell into decay, the people there were left in a deplorable condition. But at the time we are dealing with it provided employment for a number of people and added considerably to the value of otherwise sterile land.

In the Islands, but more particularly on the western shores of Inverness and Ross, fishing was an important industry, although the people had few boats capable of facing the storms of the open sea. Some, however, had small undecked boats with which they fished along the shores, and in such inlets of the sea as Loch Broom and Loch Hourn, for the shoals of herring that gathered there in the autumn. The fishing villages of Banff and Aberdeen had not yet boats sufficiently large and were not sufficiently enterprising to venture into the western sea.

The chief part of the fishing was then in the hands of the Dutch, as it had been for the previous 150 years. That enterprising maritime people had greatly encouraged this industry and sent vessels called busses, from 20 to 90 tons burden, which fished for herring in the open waters around our coasts. In the year 1618 the Dutch sent out 3,000 ships with 50,000 men to pursue this fishing, the major part of which was done on our coasts.[20] About 1688 an act was passed to compel certain Lords and Burghs to build ships, busses and boats, but this act was nullified by

---

20   Pennant 1790, Vol II, p. 371ff.

subsequent statutes which directed that no white fish be sent out of the realm, but that strangers might come and buy them. In the year 1750 bounties were promised to those who would send out busses, 50 shillings per ton being given to every buss of 70 tons, but these bounties were not promptly paid, so that many of those adventurers who had gone into this enterprise began to back out of it.

These busses must have resembled some of the vessels sent out from French ports to fish on the banks of Newfoundland. The best size was 80 tons, having eighteen men and three boats. This vessel having been anchored on the fishing bank, the fishermen in their boats proceeded to launch their nets. The herring were salted on board and thereafter exported. The Dutch continued to occupy the chief place in this fishing, having at the Shetland fishing grounds as many as two hundred busses while there were only one or two British busses present, and this continued until the Napoleonic Wars, which brought ruin upon their share in it. But while they had no boats of their own, a number of the people on the shores of these lochs found employment for a portion of the year on these herring busses.

One form of Highland industry, which fifty years later would be recognised as the chief industry of the North, sheep farming, was of almost no account then. It is scarcely mentioned. The chief product of the country then consisted of black cattle. A great trade was done in them, Sutherland sending out annually about 2,500 and Lochaber about 10,000.[21] A man's wealth was reckoned by them, a woman's dowry by the number of cows she brought. These were sold at about £3 per head as what we call store cattle, to be fed up for the butcher. These cattle were left out all winter and in the winter of 1771 great numbers died on account of the severity of the weather and there being no fodder to feed them.

Goats were more common than they are now. Johnson and Boswell, on their way alongside Loch Ness, stopped at a little hut and went in. The man to whom it belonged, a Fraser, was gone to Inverness to buy meal and only his wife was at home. 'Meal,' says Johnson, 'she considered an expensive food and told us that in spring, when the goats gave milk,

---

21 For a full account of the cattle breeding and marketing industry of the Highlands, see A.R.B. Haldane *The Drove Roads of Scotland,* 1997.

the children could live without it.' She was mistress of 60 goats which Mr Fraser of Balnain allowed her husband to keep for looking after his woods.[22]

Goats were kept for their milk, particularly when the family was too poor to possess a cow. Their milk was considered excellent for invalids and people travelled from the South to Dunkeld to drink goats' milk and whey for their health's sake. Excellent cheese was also made of their milk and of sheep's milk, for these latter were then regarded as domestic animals. They were kept for their wool and commonly folded at night. Their numbers throughout the country were few, the native breed was small and as marketable animals, they were despised. A person adept at stealing cattle, say from the Laigh o' Mosus or from the Lennox,[23] was admired; one who would steal a sheep deserved to be hung as a despicable creature.

Throughout the country it was customary to take the milk cows and goats away to the summer pasturing in the higher glens or up to the hill corries. Sometimes these shielings or *arridhs* were only a short distance from home, up the higher slopes of the mountain, but at other times they were a considerable distance away, up the recesses of some glen. After the peats were stacked in June, and the potatoes, planted in the fields, were put in order, the young people set off with their herd and their store of necessities. Usually the women, with the boys and some old men, were left to look after the milking and cheese-making until the colder weather, and the demands of the harvest, sent the herdsmen back again to their homes.

Pennant thus describes some sheilings in Jura: 'These formed a gro-tesque group; some oblong, many conic and so low that entrance is forbidden without creeping through the little opening which has no other door than a faggot of birch twigs. They are constructed of branches of trees covered with sods; the furniture a bed of heath placed on a bank of sod, two blankets and a rug; some dairy vessels and above,

---

22 Boswell 1785, p. 111.
23 I have been unable to identify the location of the Laigh o' Mosus (Lake of Mosses) but, although not named on OS maps, the Lennox clearly indicated an area of extensive grazing lands and a gathering point for cattle drovers just south of the Highland Line between Glasgow and Stirling (see Haldane 1997, p. 100 and Forbes Macgregor 1977, p. 62).

certain pendant shelves, made of basketwork to hold the cheese, the produce of the summer.'[24]

However, all this condition of things was about to be revolutionised through the introduction of sheep farming and the consequent enlarge- ment of holdings. Sheep farming was, about 1770, in its infancy in the Highlands. A few had been imported from the South into Lochaber about 1768, but only as an experiment.[25] However a beginning had been made by this time on the Breadalbane Estates. In Strathfillan the breed of black cattle had already been displaced by sheep, and soon the great deer forest of the Black Mount and the sides of Beinn Dòrain, where Duncan Ban Macintyre had sung his songs and stalked the antlered stag, were covered with sheep, to the deep sorrow of the Bard's heart. It lies beyond the limits of this paper to follow the progress of this industry and to show how it completed the revolution, begun in 1745. But there is no doubting how it transformed the mountain glens, how the old families were displaced by newcomers from the Borders, how holdings were enlarged without pity or prudence, swelling the tide of migration and emigration.

Travellers from England to Scotland in those days noted at once how bare the country was, without woods or hedges such as delighted the eye and increased the amenities of the former country. Johnson came expecting to find no wood and he took care to see very little, travelling through a country where little was to be seen. In the Islands particularly, no wood beyond some copse-wood was visible. In Mull he lost his good oak stick and was much concerned at the loss. Boswell tried to console him by remarking that he hoped whoever found it would restore it to him. 'No, no, my friend,' cried Johnson, 'it is not to be expected that any man in Mull who has got it will part with it. Consider, sir, the value of such a piece of timber here!'[26] I may add that this reflection, on the absence of woods in that island, has been the means of spurring its proprietors to much planting. At that date a good deal of planting

---

24 Pennant 1790, Vol II, pp. 246–7.
25 The introduction of Linton breed sheep spread from Callander northwards into the Loch Earn, Glen Dochart, Glen Falloch and Cowal districts at this time, followed only in the 1790s by the introduction of Cheviots into Sutherland, Rossshire and Caithness. See Haldane 1997, pp. 192–5.
26 Boswell 1785, p. 285.

The Caledonian Canal planned by William Jessop, built by Thomas Telford and completed in 1822. Photo taken near Fort Augustus in 1930. (Photo by Reginald Fry.)

had been done in Strathearn and elsewhere on the borders of the Highlands, at Balnagown in Rossshire and by the Duke of Atholl in Perthshire.

About the year 1738 larches were first planted on the Atholl Estate, five being planted at Dunkeld and eleven at Blair and from this date much larch was planted on that property. In Invernessshire Forbes of Culloden, the famous Lord President, planted extensive plantations of Scotch fir about 1740, and about the middle of that century Hugh Rose of Kilravock planted a considerable extent of moor on his estate. Such was the want of roads that the plants had to be carried on creels suspended from crooksaddles. Had Dr Johnson, however, penetrated somewhat further into the mainland of the Highlands, he might have seen extensive forests such as met the eye of other travellers who passed through Atholl, Braemar and Strathspey. Considerable stretches of mag - nificent old pinewood, remnants of the old Caledonian Forest, were still to be seen in various parts of the Highlands.

On the Grant Estates in Strathspey, as at present, there were extensive woods. A contract was made by Sir James Grant in 1728, with the York Company, to sell 60,000 and a later contract, in 1769, to sell one million choice fir trees, planted from Abernethy to Dulnan [River Dulnain], and at the mouth of the Spey many vessels were built of this wood. In the latter half of the eighteenth century quite a number of contracts were entered into to dispose of the natural woods growing in the Highland glens. In 1754, Sir Ludovic Grant was paid £1,000 for the oak trees of Ruiskich in Glenurquhart and with the money erected Castle Grant.

The development of any country, however, as Lord Lovat recognised, is largely dependent upon the means of communication. [27] We know how railways open up new lands and increase the trade and prosperity of old ones. There were no railways then to carry the traveller with ease and expedition through the wildest and most romantic parts of the High - lands; neither were there steamers to make accessible the Islands of the Hebrides.

The military roads occupied the place of the Highland and West Highland Railways. These roads, first begun by Major-General George

27 See footnote 100.

Sluggan Bridge, a part of the original Wade road from Dunkeld to Inverness, crossing the Dulnain River two miles west of Carrbridge.

Wade in 1725, penetrated the mountain land by two major routes. The western route was from Dumbarton by Loch Lomond, Arrochar, Inveraray, Glen Orchy, Kingshouse and Kinlochleven to Fort William, and thence along the Great Glen to Fort Augustus and Inverness. The more direct, central route was from Dunkeld along the valley of the Tay to Blair Atholl and over the Pass of Drumochter to Dalwhinnie; or by Crieff, Aberfeldy, Tummel Bridge and Dalnacardoch to Dalwhinnie. Here two main routes led via Ruthven Barracks, near Kingussie, along the Spey and over Slochd Mor to Inverness, or by the 2,500 feet high Corrieyairack Pass to Fort Augustus.[28] Anyone who has passed over these roads, particularly over Corrieyairack or the Devil's Staircase from Kinlochleven to Kingshouse in Glencoe, must have felt how steep were the gradients and that the military engineers might have skirted hills instead of crossing over them, but they were a vast improvement on what had preceded them. There was also a good coast road all the way by

---

28   For details of these and other military roads in the eastern and western Highlands see Wm Taylor *The Military Roads in Scotland* 1996.

The modern A9 trunk road reaching some 425 metres above sea level here over the Drumochter Pass on its way to Inverness and the North. With the mainline railway and part of the original Wade road near the village of Dalnaspidal shown to the left, it amply demonstrates the foresight of General Wade's engineering vision for opening up the Highlands.

Aberdeen, Elgin and Inverness on to Dingwall, Tain and Dornoch. Beyond these the roads were generally mountain tracks, fit only for horses. Bishop Forbes thought to take his chaise past Fort William, along the shore of Loch Linnhe to Ballachulish, but it got stuck in the first march dyke he encountered.

To the fairs, such as at Inverness, commodities were brought in skins and creels, bound on the backs of horses. Pennant mentions that the tenants of Lord Breadalbane brought coal from Perth on their horses' backs, travelling in strings, the tail of one being tied to the head of the next. Travellers being few, the places of accommodation for them along the way were very poor. Indeed, the manses were usually the places where travellers put up for the night. The inns were usually just alehouses, badly provided with comforts for anyone seeking accommodation.

At Aonach in Glenmoriston[29] Dr Johnson found a mean-looking but comfortable inn, kept by a Macqueen, but the next inn he came to at Glenelg was rather different. 'Here was no meat, no milk, no bread, no eggs, no wine. Whisky we might have and at last a fowl was caught and killed.' Out of the bed on which they were to lie jumped a dirty fellow, 'black as a cyclops from the forge'. Not caring to lie there, they got some hay and lay down on that.[30] Fortunately they did not require the hospitality of an inn again until they reached Oban, where they obtained good quarters.

Pennant describes the predecessor of the present Loch Maree Hotel, the best then on the road to Inverness. He and his companion, Mr Lightfoot, 'were complimented with a bedstead well covered with a warm litter of heath. We lay in our cloaths, wrapped ourselves in plaids and got good repose.' He adds: 'Great was our surprise to see [our guides] Mr MacKenzie and friends form their bed of wet hay or rather grass collected from the fields; they flung a plaid over it, undressed and lay most comfortably in what must have become an errant hot-bed, so blest with hardy constitutions are even the gentlemen of this country!'[31]

It is surprising to find that, at that date, several now well-known towns in the West were scarcely in existence. Oban consisted of a post office, inn and custom house and two or three scattered houses. Portree was a tolerable inn, no more. Sir James MacDonald had projected a village but it had not yet come into existence. Neither Tobermory nor Ullapool was yet built. They were the creations of the Fishery Society, which came into existence about a dozen years afterwards. The Fishery Society purchased land, gave sites for houses at a nominal fee but did not give any help towards the purchase of boats or equipment for fishing; so these towns never realised the purpose for which they were founded; they became mere 'cities of refuge' for those who were displaced by shepruns.

Before I conclude, I should like to say a word or two about the church and education at this period. I should like to remove a wrong impression conveyed by a remark of Dr Johnson's. He says in his fierce, dogmatic way: 'Through the few islands we visited we neither saw nor heard of

29   See footnote 10 for location.
30   Boswell 1785, p. 122.
31   Pennant 1790, Vol II, p. 381.

any house of prayer, except in Skye, that was not in ruins. The malignant influence of Calvinism has blasted ceremony and decency together.' One imagines from this remark that the ministers of Highland parishes had no churches to preach in. As a matter of fact, of only one island he visited was this true, the Island of Coll and that because the church of the parish was in Tiree. I think in every case there was a parish church in existence, poor enough maybe and often in bad repair but not in ruins. Only alas, the churches were too few (if today they are too many) and, several islands being at times grouped into one parish, the church was, to many of them, quite inaccessible.

In the seventeenth century huge tracts of land were formed into one parish, tracts so wide that the people could only meet together at the parish church once a year, at sacramental seasons, and in this way a large part of the parishioners might be said to subsist without religious ordinances. If the minister were faithful, he endeavoured, though often with great difficulty, to have occasional services in these distant parts of his parish; if he were moderately lazy, the people there did without worship.

Take, for instance, a parish such as Lochbroom, extending then over thirty miles to Coigach. There was no road, only a track along steep hillsides and in the face of dangerous cliffs, where one would scarcely dare to ride a pony. Or take a parish like Ardnamurchan, which stretches from Loch Nevis to Loch Sunart. In the northerly parts of it the people on the Clanranald Estate were Roman Catholic, but leaving them out of account, there is a stretch of over thirty miles, where there are three parishes now, then dependent on the ministrations of one man.

The parish of Coll and Tiree contained two islands, which are divided into three parishes now and yet these parishes are as wide as those we are accustomed to here. The parish of Kilmore in Mull and that of Kilmallie[32] in Lochaber were so wide that they have now been divided into four or five parishes. Iona, the Sacred Isle, the luminary of these western regions in olden days, had neither church nor school (not one who could read or write) in 1770. It had been like that since the

---

32 Neither name occurs now on OS maps. Tobermory, however, the town and sheltered bay in the north of Mull where the Author ministered at the turn of the century and where his four children were born, means 'Well of Mary', a link with its original parish name, Kilmore or 'the Church of Mary'. Of Kilmallie, in the Morar district, only the name of the famous port of Mallaig remains.

Reformation and was to remain like that for another forty years. It was Mr McNierl, of the parish of Lismore and Appin in Argyllshire, who first took up the cudgels against Dr Johnson's strictures. He had a church on the island and another on the mainland in Appin, but his parish stretched for another thirty-six miles.

A condition such as this did not aid the spiritual life of the people and we are not surprised to learn that superstition held them in thrall. Concerning the ministers who laboured in these parts, the testimony of travellers is without exception favourable. Dr Johnson hated Calvinism and all pertaining to it, yet he is constrained to acknowledge that: 'the people have no reason to complain of insufficient [i.e. incapable] pastors; for I saw not one in the Islands whom I had reason either to think deficient in learning or irregular in life. They had attained such knowledge as may justly be admired in men who have no motive to study but generous curiosity, or what is still better, desire for usefulness.' Such ministers as he met, Mr McQueen of Snizort and Mr MacLean of Coll, were worthy even of Dr Johnson's steel, or should I say, bludgeon. It is interesting to note that at Inveraray he met and had a dialectical combat with Mr MacAulay, the parish minister and grandfather of Lord MacAulay.

Mr Pennant gives more unqualified praise to the clergy. 'The most decent and consistent in their conduct of any set of men I ever met with of their order. Science [learning] flourishes among them and their discourse is not less improving than the table they entertain the stranger at is decent and hospitable. Few permit the bewitchery of dissipation to lay hold of them. They never sink their characters by midnight brawls, by mixing with the gaming world, either in cards, cocking [cock-fighting] or horse-races, but preserve with narrow income a dignity too often lost among their brethren south of Tweed.'[33] (Scottish stipends then ranged from £40 to £150.)

The vast majority of the people were Presbyterians; most of the lairds, however, were inclined to the Episcopal Church although they attended the parish church. In certain parts, such as the Clanranald Estates in the Islands and on the mainland, the Gordon Estates in Braemar and Lochaber, in Knoydart and Strathglass, the old Roman Catholic Church still flourished, in spite of the persecution it had to endure.

In certain other parts, the Episcopal Church, which had been estab-

---

33   Pennant 1790, Vol I, p. 173.

lished in the reign of Charles II, continued to retain the adherence of
the people. In its ritual it was little different from the Presbyterian mode
of service, but about this time the English Prayer Book began to come
into use and the worship of the church began to be assimilated to the
ritual of the Church of England. The places where it was to be found
were in north-east Aberdeenshire, in Strathnairn, in the Black Isle and
in Nether Lochaber and Ballachulish. In the last of these places, Pres-
byterianism was connected with William of Orange in whose reign it
was re-established, and the Prince of Orange's name was anathema on
account of the Massacre of Glencoe; so Episcopacy, which refused to
subscribe the oath of fealty to any but the King over the Water, naturally
retained the allegiance of the people.

What educational provision was made for the people of these glens
and islands? Usually the lairds retained a tutor for their sons while the
daughters grew up under the care of the mother, learning as many
accomplishments as she could give them, but the day of Higher Education for women was yet far away. Sometimes the children were sent to
the Grammar Schools of Inverness or Aberdeen; for example, the Laird
of Coll took a house in Aberdeen to educate his family. Dr Johnson
mentions that there were two grammar schools in Skye where boarders
were taken to be regularly educated, the price of food being from £3 to
£4 10s. a year and instruction half a crown per quarter. These were
evidently schools supported by the tacksmen and gentry of the island
for the education of their children.

In 1616 an act of the Scots Parliament ordained that there should be
a school in every parish, but no definite provision was made for the
schoolmaster's salary until 1696, when a new act required the heritors[34]
to pay him a certain salary from 100 to 200 marks (about £11). From
the earliest records of the Presbytery of Inverness, dating 1670, we see
that there were at that date parish schools in Kiltarlity and Kirkhill –
the salary of the schoolmaster at Kirkhill being a *cheldr*[35] of victual, £20
Scots (£1 15s.) and the baptism and marriage money – but in the
neighbouring Parish of Urquhart, in spite of the above Act, there was

34 landowners.
35 Probably a corruption of 'chalder', which was a dry measure equivalent to 16 bolls
of grain, etc. (see footnote 39).

no parish school until 1770. Although in many parishes the heritors for many years after 1696 ignored their obligations, by 1770 parish schools were universal throughout Scotland.

But although provision was made for the paltry salary, no definite provision was made for providing a proper house for the schoolmaster or schoolhouse for the children until an act of 1803, which stipulated that each parochial schoolmaster should be provided with a residence which was to consist of not more than two apartments, including the kitchen. If this was an advance on the past, what must that past have been? It gave rise to the saying that the schoolmaster was badly paid, worse housed and still worse fed. Both school and schoolhouse in very many cases were just black huts resembling those I have already spoken of without glass, window or chimney. The children each brought two peats for the fire and sometimes brought meal or fowls in payment of fees. On Handsel Monday, as the first Monday of the New Year was called, gifts of money were brought to the schoolmaster, and sometimes a cock-fight was held in the school, the teacher getting the dead birds.

With the extensive nature of the Highland parishes you can under-stand how few the parish school could serve. To remedy this there was incorporated, in 1709, the Society for Propagating Christian Knowledge, for the purpose of placing schools and teachers in the Highlands in places remote from the parish schools, and in the year 1770 this Society had 160 schools. Their teachers got no fees and their salaries ranged from £10 to £18 per annum. For example, Lachlan McLachlan, teacher at Abriachan, the grandfather of the late Revd Dr MacLachlan of Edinburgh, had the princely salary of £10 on which to rear and educate his family. These teachers also usually acted as catechists or lay mis-sionaries in the parish. For example, Dugals Buchanan was missionary as well as Society schoolmaster in Rannoch. Only English was allowed to be taught in the schools – parochial or Society schools – and to be spoken by the pupils, with the result in very many cases that, with the kind of schoolbooks used, English was learned in parrot-fashion, without understanding its meaning and forgotten once school was left behind.

About 1760 it dawned upon the Society that it might be of some advantage to the Gaelic-speaking inhabitants that they should be able to read the language, which alone they understood and in which the Gospel was being preached to them. The result was the publication, in

1767, of a Gaelic translation of the New Testament by the Revd James Stewart of Killin. This translation was used in their schools, and trans-lations of other works followed, and some twelve years afterwards the directors reported that their translations had been of marked utility, not only in opening the minds of the people to knowledge but in giving a greater desire to learn the English language than they had ever before discovered.

But the value of education was only imperfectly realised; where so many were illiterate, they scarcely felt the disadvantage of being unable to read or write. There were neither books nor newspapers for the poor; they had song and story to wile away the winter evenings; and the schoolmaster would write the very occasional letter sent to a son or brother away in a southern city. I think it is within the mark to say that in 1770 more than 70 per cent of the Highlanders were unable to read or write.

Much more might be written regarding the condition of things then; for example, in regard to the provision, or rather, want of provision for the poor. They were dependent on the voluntary contributions of the people, upon collections made in church. On examining my Session Books in the Parish of Kirkhill I found that an average sum of two to three shillings was distributed to each poor person in the month of August – not two shillings per week but per annum. Permission was given to beg, but how severe must the hard chill penury have been. Then in regard to mental illness, no asylums existed for the detention and care of the insane. Almost every village or township had its 'fools', so called, usually unkempt and untended, an anxiety and sorrow to their friends and often a source of danger to others (but see Chapter 3).

As communication between place and place was less frequent than today, the country was probably more free from certain epidemics, but smallpox, almost unknown now, was a terrible scourge then and it was quite common to see faces pitted with it. Vaccination had begun about 1760 but it was not yet compulsory nor readily submitted to, except in the Islands. So periodical epidemics of smallpox occurred, with a very high death rate, as many as 77 children dying in 1777 in an Easter Ross parish.

Perhaps the fascination of the past has not cast its glamour over me and I know that another might give a more pleasant picture of life in those days. But taking a conjunct view of things, I think we have reason to feel glad that our lot is cast in the twentieth and not in the eighteenth century. Both food and money are more abundant, the dread ogre of famine no longer haunts the land; roads and railways make it possible to carry the commodities of distant lands easily and cheaply to our doors. Knowledge has become the heritage of the most humble and there are opportunities, openings and facilities for advancement now which were entirely absent then. It is no longer in the bloody fields of war alone that the sons of the glens have won distinction. They have passed out into the great world and have taken their places with the foremost in the beneficent arts of peace and particularly in the heroic work of bringing Christian civilisation to many lands, as witness the exploits of Livingstone, MacKay, Stewart and Chalmers[36] – all sons of the Highlands.

---

36 While the Author's definition of the Highland region seems here rather liberal (Livingstone was from Blantyre in Lanarkshire), these four Scotsmen were among the greatest pioneers of missionary endeavour and development of civilisation in the 19th century. Dr David Livingstone (1813–73), medical missionary and explorer of Central and East Africa, discovered the Victoria Falls in 1855 and helped to abolish the slave trade. Alexander MacKay (1849–90) was trained as an engineer at Edinburgh, but gave his life to mission work in Uganda. James Stewart (1831–1905) worked in parallel with Livingstone, founding important educational institutes (see note 132). James Chalmers (1841–1901) was the first westerner to penetrate into New Guinea in the 1860s and in 1901 was killed and eaten by the local people.

Chapter 2

Life on a Strathspey Farm

In 1924 there was published a book[37] which has a particular interest to us Duthil people on account of both its subject and its author. It evinces a wide range of research in Highland matters belonging to the close of the eighteenth century. This it brings to bear upon the somewhat perfunctory accounts of a tacksman or gentleman farmer in the parish of Alvie during a period of twelve years from 1769, shedding a great deal of light upon his transactions and the manner of his life and the general conditions existing in the community with which he dealt. Any of us taking up the old account book would, I imagine, feel ourselves wandering in a dim, scarcely scrutable labyrinth but our authoress, by bringing to bear her diligently and widely garnered knowledge from many quarters, turns its crabbed figures and obscure names into a tale of vivid interest, a revelation that makes a countryside and its long dead people live again before our minds.

The authoress, Miss I. F. Grant, belonged to the old Auchterblair family, a daughter of Colonel Hugh Grant, a grand-daughter of Field-Marshal Sir Patrick Grant, a great-grand-daughter of Major John Grant of Auchterblair, and a great-great-grand-daughter of the Revd Patrick Grant, Minister of Duthil from 1778 to 1809. On her mother's side Miss Grant was descended from the Mackintoshes of Clune in Strathdearn, one of whom had been tenant of Dunachton and had written this account book which forms the foundation of her story.

This William Mackintosh possessed the small property of Balnespick on the south side of Loch Insh. As the name implies, this estate originally

---

37 The Author's manuscript begins 'Last autumn', indicating his talk was first given (to his parishioners at Duthil) in 1925. Miss Isobell Grant's book, *Everyday Life on an Old Highland Farm* was first published in 1924 and a second edition in 1981, from which full details of the original Account Book can be obtained. The reader is strongly recommended to this book for a detailed discussion and a reference to other writings on this period of Scottish social history, particularly in the Strathspey region of the Highlands.

belonged to the Bishops of Moray but in the alienation of church property after the Reformation it had come into the hands of this family of Mackintoshes. This Balnespick sold it in 1748 and he afterwards took a tack (or lease) for 'three nineteen years' of the Davoch[38] of Dunachton and Kincraig in the parish of Alvie from the Mackintosh chief of the day. He married a daughter of Grant of Cluny and died in 1784. His eldest son, Lachlan, married a niece of this chief and bought, in 1784, the estate of Clune in Strathdearn. This old gentleman was a better businessman than the usual run of those in his position at the time. He lived among his own people, an active, industrious and prudent life; was careful of his land and of his money and, while hard-headed, he seems to have been kindly and helpful – a better benefactor probably than one who might have the name of being more generous.

At a time when Highland gentlemen who could boast of blue blood in their veins were imprudently wasting, in the extravagance of petty pride, their small patrimonies and ruinously loading themselves with debt, we find him with a good income from money on loan, in addition to whatever he made off his farm. In one place he mentions sums amounting to between £2,000 and £3,000 loaned to various persons. In those times, when there were no banks and ready money was exceedingly scarce, the poorer people were often in great difficulty in procuring the loan of money when they required to buy food or when they were going on a journey or, perhaps, sending a son out into the world.

Balnespick was known throughout Strathspey as one who might be able to do a favour to them and, while the security offered could not, in many cases, have been considered very good, his confidence in his debtors appears to have proved on the whole warranted. It was not alone those who might be considered his own dependants, subtenants on the Davoch of Dunachton, that resorted to him in need, but persons from other parts of Badenoch. He appears to have always had ready money in his possession and he knew where he could advance with some prospect of being repaid. But we find him advancing money to widows where he probably expected no repayment.

One borrows from him money to buy a horse, another a cow, another the fittings of a plough, another to buy harness and iron; another when

---

38   An ancient Scottish unit of land area said to have averaged 416 acres.

he goes on a journey to Inverness or Elgin, another when his wife goes to Aberdeen (only two shillings), another when he sets out for Glasgow (this time three pounds). Most commonly these loans are given to pay for seed-corn or for meal; sometimes they are for funeral expenses and, more than once, for whisky. There were in those times quite a number of little houses where ale and whisky were sold, as many as thirteen in the parish of Alvie. On one occasion he provides a loan to a Samuel McDonoll in Killiehuntly (a farm on the other side of the river) of four pounds for whisky, of which he repaid two pounds in whisky itself.

It was a patriarchal state of society that existed then, a condition of things fostered by the kind of land tenure prevailing and the difference in social rank felt between the ordinary people and men in the position of Balnespick. Estates were let to what were called tacksmen or principal tenants. These were usually, like Balnespick himself and like his brother-in-law Grant of Cluny, cadets of the family of the Chief or Proprietor. Some of these tacks or farms might not be large, but their occupiers were regarded as gentlemen of the clan. In older times, when an estate was not reckoned by its rent-roll but by the number of men it could put into the field, these tacksmen were like the officers of a regiment under the chief as commandant. They brought each so many into the clan array and their rent was often very nominal. By the year 1770, however, things had changed greatly in the Highlands. The value of men had disappeared and each chief or proprietor was now anxious about his rent-roll. In many places rents were so raised that tacksmen like MacDonald of Kingsburgh in Skye had to emigrate. In Strathspey, on both the Mackintosh and the Grant Estates, the old families were able as yet to continue, for rents were moderate, as indeed they are still.

For Dunachton and Kincraig Balnespick paid a rent of £84, but then subtenants were due to him a like sum so that, so long as he got his rents, he had his land for nothing. On the average he only got about three-fourths of the gross rent due, but again they paid a great deal in the various services they rendered. The tacksman was the intermediary between the common people and the laird: he was indeed their laird. They had their holdings from him, paid him rent and service and were thus dependent on him. Very often they had no leases and, being usually very poor, they had not an envious position. Complaint was frequently made at that period of the harshness of these tacksmen, of their inhumanity to these subtenants, extracting the utmost from them and evicting them ruthlessly. One, writing about the condition of the High-lands in 1785, says: 'The chieftain lets out his land in large lots to the inferior branches of his family, all of whom must support the dignity of the lairds. The renters let the land out in small parcels from year to year to the lower class of people and to support their dignity squeeze everything out of them they can possibly get, leaving them only a bare subsistence.'

The system had outlived the feudal times to which it naturally belonged and it was soon to give place to a more just and economic form of tenure where subletting was abolished, the services expected were discontinued and the lowest tenants had independent leases. The tacksman became just a farmer, responsible alone for what he farmed. But in Balnespick's case, at Dunachton, we see the old system under favourable auspices, when the old Highland feeling of clanship and *noblesse oblige* was still strong and one in possession of such a tack recognised his responsibility toward those dependent on him. A great deal depended upon a man's own manner of life. If he lived extrava-gantly, as he was tempted to do by the idea of his dignity, then he was apt to act harshly; if he lived a simple life among his own people, as this man did, counting their and his own interests as one, trying to provide work for them and being ready to come to their aid in adverse years, then his value in a countryside might be very great. And in many parts of the Highlands the passing of the tacksmen was a great loss – not the system but the personalia.

Very interesting is the life of this farmhouse, as we can discern it from the jottings in his Account Book. We can see him engrossed in the seasonal operations, in his sowing and hay-cutting, in the weather and the crops, in his stock, in selling bere or oats to his tenants, in buying meal for his own house and for them, in stripping trees of bark for dyeing and carting it to Elgin; and we get glimpses of his wife equally busy at her household duties, seeing about food and work for her maids, spinning or baking or making butter and cheese. Sheep as well as cows are milked – goats are not mentioned. Some butter and cheese must have been sold, for in one account reference is made to his having at credit £22 for bark, butter or cheese.

The produce of the farm was mainly intended for home consumption.

No wheaten flour or bread ever seems to have been bought for the use of the family. Ryebread, barley-bread and oatcakes were eaten. Potatoes were used but almost as a luxury – a rare garden vegetable – for only once is there mention of them. Once they came into use, however, they speedily became the staple food of the poorer classes, ousting oatmeal from that position. The servants got six bolls[39] of oatmeal and two pairs of shoes (costing one shilling and sixpence) with their wages, about two pounds a year. From seventy to eighty bolls of meal – oat, barley, rye and some pease – were used on the house and at Martinmas two bullocks and six sheep were killed to provide meat for the winter. Fresh beef, such as we now have, could not be procured at other times. 'Kaim hens' were always plentiful.

He kept usually four menservants and a gardener, but no mention is made of maids, although probably several were kept. The latter would get two or three bolls of meal and their wages, probably one pound. But in addition to these servants the subtenants were required, without payment, to assist in ploughing and leading dung, in reaping and stacking hay and corn, in cutting peats and leading them home and in doing the long carriage: i.e., carrying produce to a distant market, as when bark was carted to Elgin. The tenants who did this work received no wages for themselves or for their horses and provided their own food. He sometimes employed a number of men bark-cutting at sixpence to eightpence a day, as many as 178 in 1770. From the sale of the bark he received nearly £30. On the swampy meadows down by the Spey he cut a considerable amount of hay, for the cutting of which he usually paid in meal. By the sale of this hay at five pence a stone, and bark at eight shillings per boll, in addition to that of cattle at two to three pounds per head and sheep at two to three shillings each, together with the sale of meal to subtenants and others, he was able to make a comfortable income.

Payment for services rendered were usually made not in money but otherwise; for example, the smith was paid in iron and meal, the shoemaker's bill was settled with a hide and the joiner's in wood. The weaver gave his services in lieu of rent and there is an amusing entry,

---

39 A boll was a dry measure, quartered into firlots and then into pecks and, depending on the density of the grain, would weigh some 8–10 stone (see Taylor 1996 p. 177).

'to the taylor and the hens one boll, two firlots of bere,' implying that the itinerant taylor did the work required of him for meal also. His purchases for the home show a considerable variety of what would be classed as delicacies. A list of these includes

3½lb tea bought in Forres @ 3s/8d, in Inverness @ 4s/6d and Kingussie @ 7s/6d
Fish [probably salt fish] from Inverness @ 3s/-d per stone
Biscuits 3s/6d; Sugar 1s/6d; Soap 9d
Port & Malaga (15s/- a dozen bottles)
Whisky from Glenlivet and Ferintosh[40] @ 1s/10d a pint

He brewed his own ale and sometimes sent some of his barley to be malted. His chief transactions, however, consisted in buying and selling corn and meal. In the bad harvests of 1771 and 1772 meal and seed corn had to be procured from Perthshire and Morayshire to keep the poor starving people alive. In 1771 he sold 37 bolls and in 1772 159 bolls, the cost to the buyers being from 18s to 20s per boll; and on this, with bad debts, he probably had a considerable loss.

He generally kept from twelve to eighteen milk cows and from forty to fifty other head of cattle. The latter were kept for at least three years before being sold, so the meat would not be over-tender. As no turnips were grown and there was little provision made for feeding them during the severe winter months, it is not surprising that they were wretchedly poor in spring, that the death toll was heavy and that his cows seem to have had only an average of one calf every second year. The number of sheep kept were few. They were mostly of the old Highland stock, small in size with fine, scanty wool, but Balnespick was apparently trying to improve his breed for in three separate years he bought twenty sheep

---

40 Although no longer found among the list of whisky producers, Ferintosh has an illustrious past. In 1689, Duncan Forbes was granted the privilege of producing whisky virtually free of duty. His son, the famous Lord President, certainly benefitted from the Privilege – at his mother's funeral in 1716 there were 10,000 people in the funeral procession, who had clearly partaken of such hospitality that no one remembered to bring along the corpse! In 1786 the Privilege was redeemed, at a cost of £22,000 to the Govenment. In 1893, another company took the name for their distillery in nearby Dingwall, but the company was liquidated in 1924 and the distillery became a bonded warehouse the following year.

The Doune, home of the Grants of Rothiemurchus and close to the Strathspey region farmed by Balnespick and his neighbours.

from the South. His whole stock consisted of less than a hundred sheep and these were treated like cattle, housed in sheep cotes and herded by the children, and about two dozen were kept for milk-sheep. Sheep dung was considered of value for manuring. With this mode of shepherding it is not surprising that the mortality was considerable, about one eighth dying chiefly, I imagine, of dirt and starvation in these foul sheepcotes. A new era opened when it was discovered that sheep were healthier and better fed when allowed to forage for themselves at liberty in the woods and hillsides.

Among the items that was a blank in Dunachton in those times was that of sport and income from shooting. Today the farm rent of that place is about £200 and the shootings are let for about £1,500. Not once is mention made of game or sport, nor is there any mention of it among the old family letters or papers. It is said that in some families a servant was employed to supply the household with salmon or venison, and among some papers left by Lachlan, Balnespick's son, is an entry stating that Donald Forbes, Dunachton Beg, had paid a debt by killing a deer and giving the skin.

Of some interest is the item of house-plenishing and personal clothing. Miss Elizabeth Grant of Rothiemurchus in her *Memoirs of a Highland Lady*, describing the domestic economy of her home in the early nineteenth century, says: 'We were so remote from markets that we had to depend very much on our own produce for some of the necessaries of life. Our flocks and herds supplied us, not only with the chief part of our food, but with fleeces to be woven into clothing, blanketing and carpets, horn for spoons, leather to be dressed at home for various purposes, hair for the masons, lintseed was sown to grow into sheeting, shirting, sacking, etc. My mother even succeeded in table linen. We brewed our own beer, made our bread, made our candles.'[41]

Although no mention is made of flax being grown, yet the mention of finer linen being got from Strathspey for shirts implies that coarser linen, as well as wool, was home produced. The maids would be kept busy spinning during the winter, by the light of home-made candles or of fir-roots from Dulnain-side. In every house the supply of blankets and sheeting was a sign of good housekeeping. The weaver's bill at Dunachton was double that of the smith's. In an inventory in the account is listed: 22 pairs of sheets, 21 table cloths, two dozen pillow cases and five dozen 'servits and handtualls'. But of even more importance in the old gentleman's eyes were his own shirts, which increase in number from 26 in 1772 to 36 in 1780, half for day and half for night. He buys four pairs of shoes, one for his wife, two for his daughters and one for himself, paying four shillings each for them and in 1773 he pays John Mackintosh, shoemaker, for 26 pairs of shoes for his family, i.e., the servants, and regards the shoemaker as still in his debt for 13 shillings 'for the half hide he got last spring'. I am afraid shoemaking would not have provided much 'kitchen' or meat for the shoemaker's family at that rate.

It is fairly evident that, however reasonable and considerate this tacksman was according to his lights, the condition of the subtenants and cottars on the Davoch must have been very poor and precarious at all times. Sir Eneas Mackintosh[42] mentions that at this period there

---

41   Elizabeth Smith (*née* Miss Grant), *Memoirs of a Highland Lady*, 1928.
42   Sir Eneas Mackintosh of Mackintosh *Notes on Strathdearn* 1774–83.

were 240 people on this land, of whom 60 could bear arms. The account book mentions forty tenants and eleven other men living on the Davoch, who were probably cottars or servants. Some of the holdings were comparatively large. His son, Lachlan, held Kincraig, a holding of 65 acres; others of 40 to 60 acres were held jointly by two or three tenants. Land was divided into ploughgates of 104 acres and oxgates of 13 acres. The larger number of holdings were of a half oxgate, i.e., of 6½ acres, and some were smaller than this. The land was let for three pounds per oxgate in the best land, down to 16 shillings in the worst.

Now the yield in a good year in the best land was three-fold for oats and four-fold for barley – that was his own return where the land was better tilled and manured than the subtenants could be – and in several years the crops were spoilt by frost and bad weather. In 1770, 1771 and 1772 there was a dead loss in oats and only a half return in bere, and the people were dependent on their crops, for there was little possibility of getting work elsewhere. Taking the years from 1769 to 1778, the amount of meal available on a half oxgate in bolls was 29, (–3), 8, 15, 24, 12, 27, 13, 12, 10, an average of 14.7 bolls.[43] But this was not all available for food for the family and it was practically all they had to live on except for the price of a stirk[44] or cow (three pounds). Out of this had to be paid everything else required.

According to Sinclair the diet of an ordinary family consisted of:

Breakfast – water gruel and bread, pottage and milk or flummery[45] and milk.
Dinner – potatoes and milk, bread and milk, sowans and milk.
Supper – potatoes, gruel or kail, except from May to August when gruel pottage and milk, with some bread.[46]

Beef, mutton and poultry were a luxury scarcely ever touched except at marriages, baptisms, Christmas and New Year. When people speak of

---

43 The Author's manuscript subtracts 8 bolls (the amount needed for resowing) from each of these values, but Miss Grant's calculations appear, to me, to have already made this allowance, so I give here the original values.
44 A yearling bullock or heifer.
45 A sweet dish, or junket, of flour, milk, eggs, etc.
46 Sir John Sinclair *General View of the Agriculture of the Northern Counties and Islands of Scotland,* 1795.

or long for the good old times, or speak of places now out of cultivation where families were once brought up in comfort, account must be taken of such facts as these. Such a mode of living to the poorest labourer would be intolerable at the present day.

Observe also that these people had to do the tacksman's ploughing and carting and, to enable them to do this, they had to keep an ox for the ploughing and a garron or pony for carting and these had to be fed by themselves. Each plough required several oxen or ponies and Balnespick was able to send 21 carts and packhorses to Elgin with bark apparently off Dunachton. Then a cow or two with some followers would be kept in order that they might have milk and be able to sell a stirk or two to pay the rent, etc. These, with a few sheep, were also required to provide manure for the land.

The housing of the people, particularly of the cotter class, must have been miserable: hovels built of stone and feal (turf) or clay, the family living in one end, the cattle in the other, often without any partition between. The fire place was in the centre of the house under a hole in the roof. The furniture would consist of one or two wooden bedsteads, a press, a deal table, a meal-chest, two or three stools, a dresser and some wooden dishes and cogs and some hornspoons.

Coming to the cultivation of the land, we must transport ourselves into conditions very different from present day methods. Changes were already taking place further south but in Strathspey and Badenoch the old system of cultivation still continued. As throughout Scotland, the land was divided into two parts – outfield and infield, that nearest the house being the croft or infield, to which all the care was devoted. Sometimes the outfield was divided from the infield by a long wall of turf or stone. The infield received all the manure but there was no such rotation of crops such as we are familiar with.

At Dunachton there was no fixed shift for crops. In other places oats and barley or bear seem to have alternated but there is little evidence of this here. The crops reared were oats – white oats and small oats (the latter a very inferior grain about half the weight of the white), barley, bear (bere or bigg) – an inferior barley, rye and some peas and potatoes. Rye was sown in small quantities. Potatoes are only mentioned once in 1774 and once (mixed with bear) in 1779. Bear was gradually giving place to barley but the proportion of white oats to small oats was less than a quarter. Sometimes we find a mixture of grain, like bear and rye, sown together, particularly in a bad year. Equally strange is to find small patches of different grains sown side to side, perhaps in the hope that some kind would be spared and come to maturity but probably because of the manner in which Balnespick's own land was intermingled with the patches belonging to subtenants.

The outfield was only partially cultivated. This part was manured by keeping sheep or cattle on it. It was then ploughed and sown for three years in succession until the crop was so poor, rush or wersh oats, that it had to lie fallow for three or even six years. No hay seed was sown and you can conceive that the so-called grass that would grow during these fallow years would consist of thistles and weeds more than real grasses. In like manner the infield, never properly cleaned, would yield a considerable quantity of weeds among the grain. As I have said, the yield in a good season was, for oats, three bolls for one sown and, for barley or bear, four or five for one sown.

Balnespick is particular in mentioning when 'by the blessing of God' he began and ended his sowing and reaping. In 1769 he began sowing his oats on 17th March and his bear on 6th May. He finished about 28th May. He began cutting his bear on 22nd September, finishing on the 30th, and his oats on 8th October, finishing on the 21st. He only got the best of his oats secured on 20th November. This was an exceptionally good year. The next year, 1770, he began sowing his rye on 13th April and oats on the 26th. He began cutting his rye on 19th September and, on the 24th, his oats. But with 'hardly four days dry till the snow came on the corns the 12th Novr. my little cropt was only housed the last of it friday 31st Novr.'[47] It was a disastrous year. In place of the 1,500 thraves (of 24 sheaves) he had only 300. In 1771 the spring was very bad. He began sowing peas on 4th April. From the 13th to the 19th there was snow and drift, then there was frost until 4th May. The harvest began on 26th September but rain and frost and snow came

---

47 This date is probably an error of Balnespick's, as he earlier records the date 'Wednesday, 19th Sepbr', which suggests his date 'friday 31st Novr.' should be the 30th. However, Balnespick also often referred to dates as 'New Style' (NS) or 'Old Style' (OS), so he may possibly be still coming to terms with the Gregorian Calendar, introduced into Britain in September 1852. See I. F. Grant *Everyday Life* 1981 pp. 174–5 (also pp. 210, 260–1).

on in the beginning of October and again it was November before another poor crop was secured. In 1774, he began sowing his rye on 18th March but did not finish sowing his bear till 20th May. 'We've had snow and frost closs,' he says, 'from the 15th December till the 22nd March,' then 'cold north winds and frequent frosts,' but with 'four days very hot' in May and, 'from the first of June constant rain and cold winds until the 17th. The meadows still covered with water. Except the four days mentioned above we've had hardly one day without wind and rain till the 4th July.'

In 1775 Loch Insh was partly frozen and the spring was stormy but it was an early harvest – 24th August to 28th September and all was in on 27th October. The following spring was delayed, with snow and rain and frosty wind from the north, and the harvest weather was also bad. In 1777 the weather was more tolerable but the spring of 1778 was again 'very cold with frost and high winds ... most disagreeable weather. Wind snow frost and rain for 22 days past.' 1779 was kinder. Of the spring he writes: 'Never did see finer season' and the harvest, on the whole, was good. Yet so stormy was the following winter that the 'cattle had to be housed'. 'From the 11th November till the end of February Loch Insh was closs frozen'; snow lay on the ground, with 'many days of most violent drift' and spring continued inclement until sowing commenced on 11th April, 1780. Unfortunately, the weather in 1782–3 (after Balnespick's Account Book finishes) was even worse, for the harvest failed entirely and the Minister of Duthil in the old *Statistical* gives an appalling description of the terrible privations of the people in this area. So it is evident that the wonderful seasons of the past belong more to the realm of imagination than of history.

The runrig system was still in vogue; that is, the land was held by several tenants in common and divided into narrow patches or ridges, from twenty to forty feet wide, with a hollow between them. At the beginning of each season these were distributed and, as what was one man's this year might be another's next year, there was no strong inducement to improve the land. In some places now uncultivated you may still see the old runrigs.

As to farm implements, while Balnespick himself may have used an iron plough, the old wooden plough would be still in use among the subtenants. This was of very clumsy construction, made of pieces of wood pinned together by wooden pins, the only iron parts being the 'coulter' and 'sock'. It was drawn by six or eight oxen and required three or four men in connection with it, one to hold the plough, another to lead the oxen, another to 'mend the land' with a spade and yet another to prod the oxen. It cost about five shillings. Harrows were also wooden, costing about three shillings. The carts used were, like the horses, small, with wooden wheels and cost about two shillings and sixpence. Horse-collars (1d.) were made of straw, halters (2½d.) of hair, traces (7½d.) of hair or hemp and saddles (6d.) of wood.

Corn was cut with a sheaving hook. The reaper was supposed to cut so many thraves, each of which was made of two stooks of twelve sheaves, and particularly where the reaper was paid by the thrave, they were inclined to make them small. A 'birleyman' (or 'proofman' elected as arbitrator by the tacksmen) tested the sheaves with a fork whose prongs were five inches apart. (I remember once, many years ago, a harvest badly laid being cut by the hook and the difficulty the grieve had in keeping the reapers to the correct size of sheaf.) Threshing was done by flail and winnowing with sieves, fans and riddles. It was a slow, laborious process but time was of less account than it is today.

During the long winters little could be done. When spring came tardily the men were kept busy ploughing and sowing, and after that peats had to be cut. In the end of May the sheep and cattle were driven over the hill to the head-waters of the Dulnain, where the shielings were. 'Blankets, foodstuffs, churns and dishes [wooden] were loaded on to carts,' says Miss Grant, 'with *caillachs* (i.e. old women) and spinning wheels on the top of them, and with lowing of cattle and barking of dogs, more than half the community would set off up the rough track that wound over the shoulder of the hill, to picnic in the rude little huts of the shielings.'[48]

The children and young women would remain under the supervision of older people until, by the end of August, the grass was eaten and the demands of the harvest made it expedient for them to return home. In the meantime the men at home had been busy peeling bark and cutting the rough grass that grew – and still grows – on the swampy meadows by the side of the Spey. By the third week of September a beginning

48   I. F. Grant 1981 p. 118.

was made with cutting the rye; then the barley and oat crop would be ready and, with uncertain and unsettled weather and the slow processes of harvesting, winter with snow would often be upon them before all was safe in stack.

Also in the autumn the South-Country drovers came, or Highland drovers brought through the countryside the cattle that were to be sold. They had now come down from the glen in good condition after their summer feed and were fit for market and the long journey to Falkirk Tryst, or to Newcastle or even further south. The breed was still the small black cattle, for as yet we see no evidence of an attempt to improve the stock. A five-year-old bullock was said to be no bigger than a Guernsey and the cows only gave about a quart of milk. Prices were beginning to improve but stirks would bring only one to two pounds and older beasts about three. Over against these prices the price of meal, when it had to be bought in (and seldom did this not occur) ranged from fifteen to twenty shillings a boll. How these people lived is a mystery to me!

Yet I warrant discontent is at any rate far more vocal today than it was then. They were marvellously cheerful folk and probably the workers sang more merrily than they now do. Every action had its lilt or chanty. The milkmaid sang at her milking, the spinner at her wheel, the women 'wauking' the cloth and the reapers in the harvest field. It must have been a pleasant sight to watch them working and singing together; and yet behind that there lay hardships of which we know nothing. A fiddler or piper would sometimes be hired to encourage the workers at peat-cutting or harvest and a dram of whisky would be given, but all that did not make up for an empty girnel [meal chest] or ill-fed bodies.

It is a mistake to imagine that the soldiers of the Highland regiments of the eighteenth century were so much taller than they are today. As a matter of fact the average was under five feet six inches. Probably the earliest recruits to the Black Watch were taller, but they were mostly of what one might call the yeoman class, not the common peasantry. Burt says: 'the common people are generally small,' and *The Statistical Account for Alvie Parish* speaks of the people as being below middle size owing to poverty and privation. It was the spirit, much more than the flesh, that created those intrepid soldiers, able to bear fatigue, to live upon little and to fight against odds.

When one looks back to such a community as existed on the Davoch of Dunachton, or indeed anywhere throughout the Highlands in the end of the eighteenth century and the first part of the nineteenth, one's chief regret is the disappearance of the old rural crafts. Several of the old home industries have entirely disappeared and, in some respects, we are less capable of helping ourselves than our forebears were. When today one rushes to a shop to buy some article, in olden times he would put his hand to making it. Where today is the ordinary man who will repair his children's boots, not to say make a new pair for them? Where in any Highland village is heard the whirr of the spinning wheel or the throb of the loom? In every village and township there was a tailor, a weaver, a shoemaker, a wright or joiner and a smith.

The aristocrat of these was probably the smith. He usually had a good croft and, as a worker in iron and in the more expensive instruments of husbandry, he acquired particular respect. The smithy was the parliament house of the community and those who depended on the smith's hospitality had to be deferential. Probably he also still enjoyed the afterglow of a past dignity as the armourer from the earlier days when men went forth from his forge with sharpened claymores. The best beloved of all the craftsmen was the tailor, who went from house to house with his board and shears and was full of song and fairy tale. The children especially had a welcome for him and sat entranced around him. My favourite of those old craftsmen was the weaver – a gentle bent figure who, working alone in semi-seclusion, had time to think and who gave me books. The shoemaker's shop was also a favourite resort; a cosy place where one watched deft operations. The joiner's shop was more awesome for we somehow thought of him only as maker of coffins.

In the community which we are considering there were two smiths, six weavers, four tailors, two shoemakers, three millers, four wrights, one cooper and a mason. They are said to be 'fit only for the coarsest work'. One Alexander Macdonald was smith and held three oxengates, or nearly forty acres of land. Between him and Balnespick there was a series of financial transactions, for he was frequently in arrears of rent and received loans of money and meal. He died in 1772 in considerable debt and Balnespick paid a considerable part of the funeral expenses in meal, whisky and sugar. He also supplied two bolls of meal to the widow, paid for a suit for her boy and, when he was sent to his uncle, sent two shillings to the uncle.

One John Campbell was a weaver and had his croft 'at the gate'. Balnespick arranged a marriage for him, but the lady and her friends did not desire the connection. The weaver, however, arranged a satisfactory marriage settlement; he agreed to pay her eight pounds 'in slump' and two pounds a year and to leave her 'his effects', so the marriage duly took place. John McIntosh was one of the shoemakers. In 1773 Balnespick paid him for 26 pairs of shoes by giving him a hide. This more than balanced the accounts, so either the hide was very large and valuable or the shoes were very cheap. One wonders how he paid his way and how many shoes he could produce from the hide. The mason was a Peter Macdonald, but evidently the demand for houses was not so great as nowadays and masons' wages were small for he was glad to get work peeling bark. Both he and his son died about the same time and Balnespick lent his widow £5 16d. to pay for their funerals.[49]

One of the most important men in the community in those days was the foxhunter. Great depredations on lambs were committed by these pests and we find Balnespick collecting from his tenants one shilling each as their share in the foxhunter's wages. Among his son's papers is an agreement between himself and Duncan Macpharlin, the foxkiller, to pay to the latter nine shillings sterling for every fox young and old that he shall kill between Ardvordan and Lagnacaillich.[50] At an earlier date (1768) a certain sum was entrusted to Balnespick to pay five shillings for every large fox killed 'betwixt the bounds of Dunachtune-more and the east end of Lynwilge'. In that year 26 were killed, so they must have been numerous.[51] Throughout the Highlands, indeed, the *brocair* with his terriers was a familiar figure and wonderfully keen experts were his little followers in rooting the foxes out of their dens, and great was the fight if they discovered not a fox but a badger.

Another craftsman mentioned is one John McPherson, a fiddler; doubtless he was accounted an important member of the community and often lent assistance, or encouragement, at hay-making time al-

---

49 I. F. Grant 1981 p. 152.
50 The editor has been unable to identify these two points, though a rocky outcrop – Creag na Caillich (see Places Index) – at the head of Glenfeshie may be an indication of their vicinity.
51 I. F. Grant 1981 pp. 145 & 275.

though neither he nor his fellow artist the piper, who is not mentioned, was esteemed for worldly prudence. Poor as a piper is proverbial.

Very poor the people might have been but they had their recreations and times of enjoyment. The principal amusements of the people in the parish according to Mr Gordon, a famous minister of Alvie, were 'camack matches, raffles and dancing'. At Christmas and New Year great games of camack, or shinty, were played not by a dozen or fifteen players on each side but by the whole manhood of each district, drawn up on opposite sides.[52] Usually a cask of whisky was provided and the keenness and excitement of the contest under the influence of 'John Barleycorn' often ended in a free fight. So the enjoyment of the day was followed by the misery and pain of sore bones and sore heads on the morrow. More pleasant was the recreation of dancing, of which the people were very fond.

A marriage was a great occasion for providing food and drink, such as were seldom partaken of at other times. Mrs Grant of Laggan speaks of being present at a shepherd's wedding where four sheep were killed. Sir Eneas Mackintosh, Balnespick's chief and landlord, describes the customs prevailing on such an occasion; how on the wedding morning 'the Bridegroom first (preceded by a Bag pipe) having a young man on each side of him, next the Bride with her two maids proceed for church. When the ceremony is over and the partys come out, pistols and guns are fired over their heads and a cake broke over the bride's head, where a great struggle is made for a piece of it. Upon their return a dinner is ready, several cows and sheep being frequently killed for that purpose. When it is over the bridegroom goes round the guests with a plate, when everyone gives according to his inclination.' Then dancing takes place to the pipe or fiddle and the fiddler receives a penny for each dance. They continue thus 'till the hour for the young peoples going to bed, when the whole accompany them to the barn, (for they are not allowed to sleep in the house the first night).'[53] The wedding continues several days, apparently until the food and drink are consumed.

---

52 In Gaelic *camanachd*, similar to the Irish game of hurling as both are played with a *caman*, or stick. Camack is said to date back some 1,500 years in the Highlands, though rules were only firmly established in 1861 by the University of Aberdeen. Kingussie is still one of the most successful clubs in the country.

53 I. F. Grant 1981 p. 131.

Deaths and funerals do not suggest occasions for enjoyment but for solemnity and sadness. It is, however, scarcely a caricature to say that the Highlander counted a funeral equal to two marriages. When a death occurred, immediately relatives and neighbours gathered to watch or wake the body. The custom sprang from the idea that for three days the spirit of the dead person hovered round the body and also that evil spirits were near, seeking to enter and must be driven away. So a good fire was kept burning, sometimes a candle was lit on the corpse and the friends sat round and told ghost stories. Whisky and snuff went around and under their influence very often the solemnity vanished and the occasion became one of enjoyment. Miss Grant of Rothiemurchus tells how, when old Gerry Ross, the hen-wife's husband, died, 'he was waked after the old fashion, shaved and partly dressed, and set up in his bed, all the country side collecting round him. After abundance of refreshment the company set to dancing, when, from the jolting of the floor out tumbled the corpse into the midst of the reel and away fled the guests screaming that he had come to life again.'[54] At any rate it awed the revellers.

From Balnespick's Account Book one can see what a serious item was the expense considered necessary in connection with a funeral. Advances of one to two pounds are made by him to widows to provide meal and whisky for the funeral feast. It is not surprising that sometimes men returning from a funeral looked very unlike those who had been engaged on a sad errand and that the burials sometimes tended to resemble heathen orgies rather than a Christian service.

These past times with their vanished customs have a certain fascination for me, or at least for a certain part of me – I sometimes imagine that the blood of some old *seanachie* must be in my veins. But as you may infer, I am no *laudator temporis acti*, no flatterer of past ages. I am inclined to think that, taking a balanced view, conditions are better in Strathspey in our own day than they have ever been. When we compare them with those I have so imperfectly described, while mountain, loch and river remain unchanged in all their picturesque beauty and human nature itself is little altered, yet we seem to live in another region of life. Sometimes rural communities are reproached for being slow to alter habits and systems of

---

54   Elizabeth Smith 1928 p. 192.

working; slow to learn and adapt themselves to better ways of cultivation and improved methods of living, slow to discard what has only traditional habit to recommend it. But, while one regrets the passing of the old-time craftsmen and home industries, the nineteenth century brought to the Spey valley a period of improvement, without the horrible disfigurement of our landscape and the creation of such unnatural and unhealthy conditions of life as have occurred elsewhere.

Our farmers, working under frequently unfavourable conditions, have exhibited a laudable enterprise and, although harvests are still precarious, the altered methods of crop rotation add to the great advantages of new means of transport, while vastly improved stock in cattle and sheep have driven the ogre of hunger and want away from the doors which once he haunted. Dr Johnson, writing about 1775, speaks of being repelled by the barren wilderness of nature in the Highlands. 'The appearance,' he says, 'is that of matter incapable of form and usefulness, dismissed by nature from her care and disinherited of her favours. It will readily occur that this uniformity of barrenness can afford very little amusement to the traveller; that it is easy to sit at home and conceive rock and heath and waterfalls and that these journeys are useless labours, which neither impregnate the imagination nor enlarge the understanding.' Burt, in his letters, speaks of 'the huge naked rocks producing the disagreeable appearance of a scabbed head. To the east, if one casts one's eye from an eminence towards a group of them, they appear one above another, fainter and fainter and the whole of a dismal gloomy brown, drawing upon a dirty purple, and most of all disagreeable when the heath is in bloom.'[55]

It seems scarcely credible that these men should be so insensible to the grandeur of the Highland scenery. All this insensibility has passed and now the places that seemed so gloomy, so repellent, so horrid, so destitute of nature's charm have become centres of attraction and delight to multitudes.

---

55   Capt. Edmund Burt *Letters from a Gentleman in the North of Scotland* 1754, reprinted
1974, p. 282.

Chapter 3

The Highland Fool

''s minig a thainig Comhàirle ghlic a Beul Amadain'
('Oft has the wisest advice proceeded from the mouth of folly')
Thomas Pennant, 1790[56]

A distinguished general, who had left the Highlands in his youth for service in India and who returned many years afterwards to his native land, said to a friend with great seriousness: 'Will you believe me when I tell you that among the many things so long associated with my faithful remembrances, that have passed away and which I miss much, are – pray, don't laugh at me when I confess it – my old friends the fools.' 'And,' said Norman McLeod relating the incident, 'I heartily sympathise with the General.'[57]

About a hundred years ago one could scarcely pass through a village or town in Scotland without seeing and meeting with persons whose sanity was evidently somewhat defective. Our modern asylums[58] have gathered into themselves and withdrawn from public gaze most of that unhappy class whose mind is lacking in certain constituents of a rational under-standing. Sometimes one still meets with the 'village fool', some innocent with a vacant smile upon his face or some crazed wanderer who moves restlessly from place to place with strange imaginations peopling his brain. These are the dying remnant of a numerous company that was once to be found; objects of pity or sorrow or amusement in every district of Scotland.

---

56 From his collection of Gaelic Proverbs in *A Tour in Scotland & Voyage to the Hebrides*, 5th edition, 1790.

57 Dr Norman McLeod *Reminiscences of a Highland Parish* 1871, footnote to p. 320.

58 The modern reader should note that recent health legislation, under the title 'Care in the Community', has reversed this trend of institutionalising the mentally ill or handicapped person, though hopefully with more concern and provision for their day to day welfare. It remains to be seen how effective this is in creating a greater sympathy of understanding and acceptance.

Some of them were indeed a sad spectacle to look at; creatures weak in body and idiotic in mind, usually ragged and dirty, unattended to and incapable of attending upon themselves; miserable objects for which no adequate relief existed; often thrust out by their own friends to be at night in some dark and wretched corner and in the day sent out to beg for scraps of food. When passing through a village, in all likelihood they would be followed by a crowd of children who found a cruel pleasure in badgering and tormenting them, in shouting opprobious epithets at them. And at times these poor defective or demented creatures would turn, like hunted beasts at bay with wild eyes and wilder words, threatening their tormentors.

But beside that lower class of the crazed and cretinous, for which modern legislation has made merciful provision, there was a less pitiable class: the fools or half-wits whose disappearance that old general regretted; whose strange tales of adventure or unexpected flashes of wit added considerably to the amusement of the people among whom they dwelt. This type of person was, as Shakespeare said, 'a pleasant fellow i' faith with his brains somewhat in disorder.' 'These fools were,' says Dean Ramsay,[59] 'eccentric or somewhat crazy, idle creatures, who used to wander from house to house and sometimes made shrewd, sarcastic remarks upon what was going on in the parish. They used to take great liberty of speech regarding the conduct and disposition of those with whom they came in contact.' 'The Highland fool,' says Dr Norman McLeod in his *Reminiscences of a Highland Parish,* 'was the special property of the district. He was not considered a burthen upon the community, it was felt a privilege to assist him. He wandered at his own sweet will wherever he pleased, ower the muir amang the heather, along highways and byways with no let or hindrance from parish beadles, rural police or poor law authorities.'[60]

He was usually considered a privileged guest and considered himself such a guest at whatever house he chose to visit. He generally took good care that this was a house where he could get plenty of food, a good kitchen fire to warm himself beside and a cosy barn, with plenty of clean straw to make his bed in. He had thus a partiality for manses

---

59   Dean Ramsay *Reminiscences* 1924, pp. 249–50.
60   McLeod 1867, p. 297.

and for the houses of substantial farmers. There he was usually cheerfully welcomed by the servants, the lads and lasses who gathered on winter nights round the big ingle with its blazing logs. Here he held a kind of levee, while he told the latest news of the countryside, or related some extraordinary adventures through which he had passed, or uttered some remark of caustic sarcasm at the expense of someone present or some simple, laughter-provoking saying that put all in good humour with him.

In older days than those I particularly refer to, 'a professed fool was considered a necessary appendage to every family of distinction.' The king had his jester and the chief or laird, great or small, had to have his fool whose character was usually composed of wit, knavery and simplicity. Up to the end of the eighteenth century and sometimes even later it was quite common to find attached to a laird's household some half-witted individual who repaid kindness by sterling fidelity and devotion to the family. He was useful in going errands and carrying messages from one 'big house' to another in days before the facilities of our present postal system were dreamt of.

When the demand for 'family fools' was great, and when these functionaries were well provided for, it became necessary to check the assumption of this character by unscrupulous knaves. An old Scottish act of Parliament, with the title 'Act for the way-putting of fenyet fules',[61] enacted and ordained that sheriffs, bailies and officials should enquire at every court 'gif there be ony that makes them fools that are nocht; and gif ony sic be fundyn, that thai be put in the King's ward or in his irons for their trespass as long as they have ony gudes of their awn to live upon, and when they have nocht to live upon, that their ears be nailit to the trou or to ane uther tree and cuttit of and they bannishit the cuntre; and gif thereafter they be fundyn again, that they be hangit.' Sufficiently drastic and, one might suppose, effective measures!

Sometimes, indeed, it seems hard to believe that this or that saying, so apposite, so shrewd, so caustic can have been uttered by a person classified among the mentally deficient, just as the cunning at times shown by these persons tempts one to imagine that they were more

---

61   19th January 1449.

rogue than fool. But one of the essential characteristics of wit is unexpectedness. Dullness, absence of feeling, absent-mindedness suddenly giving place to a startling alertness and quickness is a frequent source of laughter. See a staid, stout man suddenly running after his hat and you can scarcely forbear laughing at him. Hear some dull, vacant-eyed individual suddenly utter a quick repartee and your astonishment will enhance your amusement.

What has made the sayings of many a fool memorable is this startling element of unexpected aptness and wisdom. Take, for example, the saying of a half-wit I once knew. This man used to work, when the mood possessed him, with his father in the slate quarries at Ballachulish. One day a number of men were standing at the quarry gates, waiting for the work bell to ring, and began discussing Gaelic poetry of the elegiac type. One of the men, Donald V, rather an unsteady workman and a bad payer, said to the others: 'Well, lads, I think an elegy is a fine thing, I would like to be remembered after my death; I would like someone to compose an elegy (a *marbhrann*) on me.' John, the half-wit, was standing in his usual listless attitude, gazing with open mouth and eyes up into the sky and apparently inattentive to what was going on around him, when all at once he turned to Donald and said: '*Bithidh marbhrann (cuimhneachain) gu leòr ortsa ann an leabhraichean an Stòir.*' ('There will be sufficient memorial to you in the books of the Store.')

Or take another example from the life of Jamie Fleeman, the famous Aberdeenshire (Laird of Udny's) fool.[62] At a certain harvest home at which he was present, the farmer's daughter invited him to dance with her. Fleeman, proud of being so honoured, immediately stood up when her mother, thinking that the whole family would be disgraced by the girl's frolic, forbade her. While she was scolding her daughter for her low behaviour, some of those present interfered and sought to persuade her that there would have been no harm in dancing a reel with Jamie. 'Let the auld owman alane,' said Jamie with a sarcastic air, 'sae nae mair about her; she is God's handiwark.'

So many of our Scottish stories of wit and humour are connected with my own profession that it is not surprising to find that a number of witty fools' sayings relate to their encounters with ministers. The fool

---

62   *The Life and Death of Jamie Fleeman, the Laird of Udny's Fool*, 1810.

was always fond of going where a concourse of people was to be found. In the important funeral processions of those days he usually took to marching at its head, and on the Sabbath he might be found in the front seat of the laft, making faces at the minister or, as likely, at the very foot of the pulpit stairs.

Once, in the church at Maybole, when Dr Paul, afterwards minister of St Cuthbert's,[63] was officiating, the fool John McLymont stood so close to the pulpit door as to overlook the Bible and desk. When asked to stand back a little, he got intensely angry and exclaimed: 'Sir, maybe I'll come further,' meaning of course that, if provoked, he might enter the pulpit itself. That happened in the case of another. One morning, when the minister entered his church, he found his pulpit already occupied by 'daft Tam' and the elders trying in vain to induce him to vacate it. On seeing the situation the clergyman cried out in a peremptory tone: 'Come down out of that immediately, sir.' 'Na, na, minister,' answered Tam, 'just ye come up wi' me. This is a perverse generation and faith they need us baith.'[64]

Once in the parish of Lunan, in Forfarshire, the minister took occasion to reprimand his people for sleeping in church – a habit that appears to have been more common in past days than at present. Noticing how wakeful and apparently attentive was the parish fool, Jamie Fraser, who occupied the front seat in the laft, while worthy farmers were snoring on either side of him, the minister stopped in his discourse and spoke straight to them. 'You see,' he exclaimed, 'even daft Jamie Fraser does not fall asleep as you do.' Jamie, by no means relishing this unflattering designation, coolly replied: 'Aye and I hadna been daft, I wad hae been sleeping too.'

Another of those characters belonging to Peebles was one day sitting in church listening attentively to a strong denunciation from the pulpit of the evils of deceit and falsehood. He was observed to grow uneasy, to begin to fidget in his seat, to grow red in the face and at last he roared: 'Deed, Minister, there's mair leears in Peebles than me.'

Many are the anecdotes told of encounters between these half-wits and ministers in which the divine comes off second best. Here are two

---

63   Church of Scotland, Lothian Rd, Edinburgh.
64   Ramsay 1924 pp. 250–1.

which Sir William Chambers gave to Dean Ramsay for his reminiscences.[65]

Daft Jock Gray, the original of Scott's Davie Gellatley, was reproved on one occasion by a rather pompous South Country minister for his idleness. 'John,' said the minister, 'you're a very idle fellow. You might surely herd a few cows.' 'Me, hird?' replied Jock, 'A dinna ken corn frae gerse.'

Almost too sharp and caustic to be the utterance of a fellow of defective mental powers was the encounter between old Dr Auld of Ayr – Burn's 'Daddy Auld'[66] – and daft Rab Hamilton. One day, as Rab waited for the minister, expecting a coin, the latter hurried past him saying: 'Get away Rab; I have nothing for you today.' 'When, when,' cried Rab in a half-whining tone, 'I dinna want anything the day, Maister Auld; I wanted to tell you an awesome dream I hae had. I dreamt I was died.' 'Well, what then?' said Dr Auld. 'On I was carried up, up till I came to heavens gett where I chappit and chappit and chappit till at last an angel looked oot and said: "Wha are ye?" "Ain puir Rab Hamilton," says I. "Whur are ye frae?" says he. "Frae the wicked toon o' Ayr." "I dinna ken ony sic place," said the angel. Well, he sends for the apostle Peter and Peter comes wi' his key and opens the gett and says to me: "Honest man, do you come frae the auld toon of Ayr?" "Deed do I," says I. "Well," says Peter, "I ken the place but naebody's came this wey frae the toun of Ayr, no since the year 17—"' [mentioning the year when Dr Auld was inducted into the parish].

I remember a half-wit in my native parish one day meeting a worthy Free Church minister and saying to him: '*Càit an do chuir sibh na searmoin deuchainn agaibh? Chan eil sibh a' toirt a leithid dhuinn an nis idir.*' ('Mr McCallum, where have you put your Trial Sermons? You never give us the like of them nowadays.')

Another minister friend of mine was celebrating his semi-jubilee and his congregation, noting the somewhat worn state of the pulpit Bible and Psalm Book, resolved to commemorate the occasion by presenting

65 Ramsay 1924, pp. 254 & 260.
66 Sometime in 1781 Robert Burns was publically called by Dr Auld to do penance for fathering an illegitimate child. His response was to write a number of satirical poems, including 'Epistle to Ranken' and 'Poet's Welcome to an Illegitimate Child' (J. G. Lockhart *Life of Robert Burns* 1907 p. 32.)

him with new books. For this purpose some of them went round soliciting subscriptions. Among others who were asked to contribute was a certain John who, like many another half-wit, was fond of music of a kind. John, shortly before this, had managed to acquire a set of bagpipes on which he was accustomed to play certain tunes of his own, to the delight of his mother whose own mental capacities were little better than his. 'You're going to give me something, John?' said the collector. 'No!' answered John. 'Well, but I hear you were buying bagpipes lately.' 'Yes,' was the reply, 'and me and my bagpipes will be of more service hereafter than the Minister and his books.' 'How can that be?' exclaimed the worthy collector in astonishment. 'To waken the dead!' said John as he turned on his heel.

Some of these simple folk were fond of relating extraordinary adventures which, they alleged, had happened to themselves. They permitted their imagination to run riot while they evidently persuaded themselves that their tales were true. No greater delight could be afforded to boys and girls, lads and lasses than to sit around the wide kitchen hearth and listen to Daft Jamie or Jock as he poured out, in reply to a few leading questions, the record of his extraordinary feats or his wonderful voyages and his encounters with birds and beasts and fishes. Beside some of these tales those of Jules Verne or of H. G. Wells would seem tame and insipid.

Dr Norman McLeod, in his *Reminiscences of a Highland Parish*, mentions one of these fools, Donald Cameron by name, who was accustomed to draw the long bow with considerable skill. 'Donald,' says Dr Norman, 'was never more brilliant than when narrating his submarine voyages and his adventures as he walked along the bottom of the sea, passing from island to island. He had an endless variety of stories about the wrecks which he visited in the caverns of the deep and, above all, of his interviews with the fish, small and great, whom he met during his strange journeys.

'"On one occasion," I remember his telling me with grave earnestness as we sat fishing from a rock, "I was sadly put about, my boy, when coming from the island of Tiree. Ha! Ha! Ha! It makes me laugh to think of it now, though at the time it was very vexing. It was very stormy weather and walking was difficult and the road long. I, at last, became very hungry and looked out for some hospitable house where I could get rest and refreshment. I was fortunate enough to meet a turbot, an old acquaintance, who invited me most kindly to a marriage party which was that day to be in his family. The marriage was between a daughter of his and a well-to-do flounder. So I went with the decent fellow and entered a fine house of shells and tangle, most beautiful to look upon. The dinner came and it was all one could wish. There was plenty to eat and drink, for the turbot had a large fishing bank for himself to ply his trade on. He had also been very industrious, as indeed were all his family, so he had good means.

"'But as we sat down to the feast, my mouth watering, who should come suddenly upon us with a rush but a tremendous cod, that was angry because the turbot's daughter had accepted a poor thin flat flounder instead of his own son, a fine red rock–cod? The savage rude brute gave such a fillip with his tail against the table that it upset. And what happened, my dear, but that the turbot, with all the guests – flounders, skate, haddock and whiting, thinking I suppose that it was a whale, rushed away in a fright and I can tell you that, when I myself saw the cod's big head and mouth and staring eyes, with his red gills going like a pair of fanners and when I got a touch of his tail, I was glad to be off with the rest. Fortunately I was near the point of Ardnamurchan where I landed in safety and got to Donald McLachlan's house wet and weary. Wasn't that an adventure!'"[67]

About 1850 among the characters that might be met on the streets of Thurso was one Neil McKay, usually called '*Bonstie a' Bushans*', who delighted in relating his own exploits. Near Holborn Head is a massive stack, or rock, called the Clett. It stands out in the sea a distance of perhaps eighty yards from the main wall of cliffs. Bonstie solemnly declared that he had once, holding a sack of meal in his teeth, leapt clean over from the headland on to Clett. The return, however, was more difficult. 'I couldna get a runnin leap,' he explained, 'but when half way over I gied anither spring and landed on Hobran Heed.'

On another occasion he described his experiences at sea in these terms: 'I wis a sailor since, Jewel. I wis eichteen year at sea and three year o' 'at I nivver saw daylight. Ae day a terrible storm cam' on and the cappin sed till me: "Hae, ye black souros, tak'ir and do wi' 'ir fat

67   McLeod 1867, pp. 307–9.

ye like." So I pit 'e men under hatches and lash't masel til 'e helem. I steere 'ir intil a place 'at 'ey ca' Bellpoint.[68] It was a terrible cowld plaen, Jewel. It wis 'at cowld 'at me feet wis frozen till 'e deck and I had to rin and get bilin water til lowse them.'

I remember someone of this kind possessed of a most magnificent imagination. Someone happened to mention the size of some large turnips. 'Did you ever see anything like that, James?' asked one of the company. 'O ay,' he answered. 'When I was a lad, away at the herding, my master came one winter day round with a friend to where I was herding some sheep. "Where are the sheep, James?" he called to me. I put my fingers in my mouth and whistled and at once they appeared. Ye see, they ate the heart of the turnips and then lay down inside.'

A company of tailors were once employed at a house at which Jamie Fleeman chanced to arrive and they resolved to draw him out, in order to have a merry evening. One of them, addressing a companion, averred that, shutting his eyes, he could thread the finest needle half a dozen times in a minute. The other declared that, holding his hands behind his back, he could do the same. The master tailor, in a taunting tone, addressed Fleeman. 'Could you thread a needle, Jamie?' Immediately, he replied with some warmth. 'Ye would like to ken, would ye, tailor? Last winter, man, as I was passing Garpalhead,[69] a ship was lying on the sands. She had been ca'd in by the storm and she was loaded wi' needles. There were two men wi' shovels throwin' them out. Faith, I wis wae to see sic a loss o' fine sharps. And spyin' a greet clue o' sina thread lying, I fell a threadin' the needles and I threadit as fast as the men could sho'el them out and I didna miss ane. That was a threadin' for ye.'

Of course, there have been fools and fools. Some have left behind them only one or two sayings; others again are remembered because of a number of anecdotes regarding them, of a number of sayings and doings that still move us to smile. Certain districts of Scotland have had notable

---

68 It seems impossible to identify this Point; many headlands or rocks in olden times had bells on them, rung by the wind, as a warning to ships – the precursor of the modern fog-horn.

69 The editor can find no trace of this headland, except perhaps as a corruption of Garness Head near Banff (though with no sandy beach nearly), Garron Point further to the east or Garmouth near the mouth of the Spey.

fools connected with them and even now, long after their deaths, their remembrance is kept green.

Probably the best known of modern Scottish fools is the one whose name I have already alluded to – Jamie Fleeman. His life and sayings have been published and have enjoyed great popularity, particularly in the north-east of Scotland, my edition being the 67th thousand printing. Fleeman is usually called the Laird of Udny's fool because, while he moved through the countryside, he attached himself in an especial manner to the house of that Laird and made his home there, receiving for a considerable period a peck of meal and a sixpence per week and, occasionally, cast off clothes. He acted as a kind of errand or orra boy about the castle, bringing in peats and water for the maids or carrying letters for the ladies.

It is natural that almost every good story of which a fool has been the hero should be fathered on Jamie, just as every act of injustice done by the chief of some clan is traditionally ascribed to a particular chief, more notorious for wrong-doing, rather than others whose names are forgotten. Most of his sayings are so well known that I will cull only one or two of those I consider the best, apologising for their familiarity, as the actor did when called to play the character of Hamlet.

The Laird of Waterton was held by Fleeman in particular aversion. One day, as Jamie was lolling on a bank of the Ythan, basking himself in the sun, he was hailed from the other side of the water by the Laird who asked him which was the best ford. The malicious knave directed him to the deepest pool in the river and, in attempting to cross it, the Laird was nearly drowned. When he reached the other side he made for Fleeman and, in a voice hoarse with passion and cold water, asked what he meant by trying to drown him. 'Gosh be here, Laird,' said the fool with an accent of perfect innocence, 'I've seen the geese and the ducks hunners of times crossin' there; and I'm sure your horse has langer legs than they.'

Another day a gentleman, whose drollery outran his prudence and who, perhaps, thought that his rank gave him a title to address an inferior in any terms he pleased, met Fleeman and asked him: 'Who's fool are you?' Jamie, eyeing him for a moment with a cold stare, coolly replied: 'I'm Udny's fool. Wha's feel are ye?'

On one occasion, he had been sent to fetch some geese from Haddo House[70] to Udny Castle. Finding the task of driving them rather an arduous one, he procured a straw rope and twisting this round their

Udny Castle near Aberdeen, around which many of the tales of Jamie Fleeman, the
'Laird of Udny's Fool' are wound.

necks he dragged them after him. What was his horror on nearing his
destination and looking back at his charges, to find them all strangled.
With the cunning of his kind he devised a means which he thought
would be effective in shifting the blame from himself. He dragged his
victims into the poultry yard, stuffed their throats with food and then
boldly entered the Castle. 'Well Jamie,' he was asked, 'have you brought
the geese?' 'Aye have I.' 'And are they safe?' 'Safe? They're gobblin,
gobblin, gobblin as if they hadna seen meat for a twalmonth. I'se warrant
they're safe enench if they haena choked themsells.'

A somewhat similar ingenuity was displayed by him on another
occasion when, loitering one day in the passage leading to the dining
room as the maid was carrying the dinner, and smelling the savoury
odour of a couple of roast duck, he pounced upon the 'ashet' on which
they lay, tore off a leg of each and hid them under his coat. The maid,

70 1731 home of the Earls (later Marquises) of Aberdeen; acquired by the Secretary
of State for Scotland in 1978, to be managed by the National Trust for Scotland.

observing what he had done, insisted on his carrying the dish to the table. 'These are queer ducks,' said the laird. 'The deucks?' muttered Fleeman, 'What's the matter wi' the deucks?' 'Why, they have only one leg each.' 'Ae leg. Och, there's nacthing queer about that. If ye look oot o' the window ye'll see the deucks in the yaird in dizzens, standing on ae leg and what shouldna these twa beasties hae but ae leg tae.'

One year, when the Laird of Udny attended the Perth races, Jamie accompanied him. Taking a short cut across the fields, he reached the town before his master and somehow managed to get hold of a large portion of a leg of mutton. This he hid under his jacket till he came back to the bridge near the town, when he sat down on the parapet and began munching the meat. He did this with a great air of haughtiness, evidently feeling that he was lunching like a lord. As his master rode up, he exclaimed: 'Aye, Fleeman, are ye here already?' 'Oh ay,' with an air of assumed dignity and archness, while he glanced significantly at the mutton. 'Oh ay, ye ken a body when he hes onything.'

In the *Memorials* of the Earls of Eglinton[71] mention is made of a fool, usually called 'Daft Will Speir', who must have closely resembled Fleeman and who was a privileged person about Eglinton Castle and grounds, while also attending to certain humble duties about the kitchen. One day he was discovered by the Earl taking a short cut by crossing a fence in the demesne. The Earl cried out: 'Come back, sir, that's not the road.' 'Do you ken,' replied Will, 'whaur I'm gaun?' 'No!' said the Earl. 'Then hoo dae ye ken whether this be the road or no?'

Another day, Will was passing the minister's glebe where haymaking was in progress. The minister asked him if he thought the weather would keep up. 'Weel,' said Will, 'I canna be sure but I'll be passing this way the nicht and I'll ca' in and tell ye.'

'Well, Will,' said his master to him one day after he had come in from his dinner, 'have you had a good dinner today?' 'Och, vera gude,' was the reply, 'but gin onybody should ask if I got a dram after't, what will I say?'

One of Will's duties appears to have been, like Fleeman's, to bring into the house sufficient supplies of fuel and water. In course of time, Will was seized somewhat suddenly by severe illness which was evidently

71 Wm Fraser, *Memorials of the Montgomeries, Earls of Eglinton* 1859.

'unto death'. The minister came to see him and asked if there were not something that gave him consolation in his sore trouble. 'Aye,' gasped the poor weakling, 'the Lord be thankit, a' the bunkers are fu'.'

Most of these half-witted creatures were wanderers from house to house throughout a district. As long as father or mother were alive they might make that a kind of home, but it was seldom they remained there for any time, finding oftentimes more pleasant and comfortable quarters in the outhouse of some mansion or farmhouse; finding also the company more agreeable and the fare more abundant, for in those more hospitable days there were always scraps set aside for the beggar and the wandering fool. One of these wanderers, about fifty years ago, was connected with the Black Isle and well known in the neighbourhood of Beauly and Inverness.[72] He was called *Fearchair a' Ghunna* (Farquhar of the Gun).

Farquhar MacLennan was born in Strathconon in 1784, the son of a crofter. At the end of the eighteenth and beginning of the nineteenth century smuggling was at its zenith in the Highlands; in fact, many a crofter depended on it for payment of his rent, and Farquhar used to tell proudly how he was descended from the smugglers of Strathconon.

It is told that, when he was but a lad, his father sent him to Strathpeffer for a bag of barley seed. Returning somewhat late and finding everyone in bed, Farquhar, acting on his own version of the proverb – 'never leave off till tomorrow what can be done today' – proceeded to sow the barley. Although the people of Strathconon were not early risers, their fowls were and every hen, chicken and cock within reach of Farquhar's newly sown barley was pecking at it for hours before the household had left their beds. By that time most of the barley had disappeared. When his father chided him for sowing the barley, Farquhar replied: '*Esan aig am bitheadh bàrr math agus /foghar luathrach feumaidh (abachadh tràth dh'fheumadh) e bhi èirigh mochthrath. Nam biodh tu air eirigh tràth 'sa mhaduinn agus an talamh a chliathadh cha bhitheadh na h-eoin air an siol ithe.*' ('He who would have a good crop and an early harvest must be up betimes. Had you harrowed the ground, the fowls would not have eaten the seed.')

It appears that more than one place of service was found for the lad but he could not retain them, nor could farmers be expected to have

72   Close to the Author's parish (1908–12) of Kirkhill.

patience with his ways, so he became a wanderer, chiefly in the district contiguous to the Beauly Firth. For a time he made his home in an outhouse adjoining Killearnan Manse, but having quarrelled with the minister, whose dog he had killed, he was turned out of that and found a refuge in a hut on the Muir of Tarradale, which he called 'the Garrison'.

The most conspicuous peculiarity about Farquhar was his dress. He wore a blue Kilmarnock bonnet, replaced in later years by a wideawake hat, into which a profusion of feathers, bits of paper and other ornaments were stuck. This headgear was kept in place by a substantial iron chain. His clothes, which were nondescript in character, were secured by another iron-wire girdle passing round his body. Tied to this was a brace of old pistols, a Mexican powder horn, several hoops, bits of chain and keys. He was accustomed to pick up in his wanderings all sorts of odds and ends: old metal, bones, rags, feathers, etc. and these were usually tied about him in some way or other, so that his appearance was most fantastic. He always carried the barrel of a gun, sometimes several barrels tied together, for which he had made a rough stock. So accoutred, he regarded himself not as a wandering beggar but as a gentleman sportsman or hunter.

While evidently deficient in mental calibre, Farquhar had always a ready, and often apt answer which showed that he was not quite as silly or fantastic in mind as he looked. One of the Rossshire lairds was once anxious to attach him to his house as his own fool but Farquhar flatly refused his offer of hospitality. 'I will stay in no man's house longer than I choose,' he exclaimed. 'I am a *sealgair* [hunter] as you know and I will *siubhlaidh* [travel] through the country with my gun like all other gentlemen.'

All his sayings were uttered in Gaelic, for he knew not a word of English. He was wont, however, to go to the English service at church. On being asked why he did so, seeing he understood not a word, he answered: 'I am trying to be like my equals, the rest of the gentlemen in the country. There is no pride in going to hear a Gaelic sermon to which only common people listen.'

Once, at Muir of Ord market, he went up to two gentlemen with a request for money to buy some powder for his gun – his usual manner of begging alms. Finding them irresponsive he pointed to a stranger, an English gentleman he had seen with them, and told them he wished to ask their friend for some but, as he did not know English, he did not know what to say to him. '*Rach suas thuige* (Go right up to him),' said one of them, '*Cuir do ghunna ris agus abair* (Present your gun to him) and say: "Guard your life!" and he will give you *fùdar gu leòr* (plenty of powder).' Farquhar went up to the gentleman, presented his gun and in his usual gruff manner said: 'Guard your life!' and, not surprisingly, the man thus accosted turned upon his heel and made his way out of the market as quickly as his legs could carry him.

Farquhar, on one occasion, was passing along a road when he saw, on the moor above him, an animal browsing. He at once charged his gun, cautiously stalked the animal and when he had come within a reasonable distance, applied the match in his usual manner to the touch-hole and 'bang' went the shot. The quadruped was not harmed but, alarmed at the report, ran away with Farquhar in hot pursuit. It at length made its way to a house some distance off, still with the hunter at its heels. 'Hello!' cried the occupier of the house. 'Why are you running after my ass?' "*S e th'ann damh a loisg mi air air a' mhonadh agus tha mi air a bhith ruith as a dheidh fad an latha*,' was the reply. ('It's a stag that I shot on the hill, and I've been after it the whole day.')

When Farquhar was in possession of an outhouse near the Manse of Killearnan, he collected in it a mass of metal, stones, bones, rags, rooks and frogs, which did not improve the savour of its atmosphere. One day, the Revd Mr MacRae peeped into this abode and cried: '*Fuigh! Fuigh! 'S ann agad tha 'm fhàileadh asad Fhearchair!*' ('Faugh! Faugh! What a bad smell you have, Farquhar!') At once came the retort: '*Tha iad ag innse adh dhomh gu bheil fhàileadh math aig na fèidh ach tha fhàileadh nas fhearr agadsa nuair a fhuair thu fhàileadh stiopain a' Chaisteil Ruaidh bho Ameireaga.*' ('They tell me that the deer have a keen scent but you had a keener when you scented the Redcastle stipend from America.') The reverend gentleman had come from America shortly after the Disruption and had been presented to the charge rendered vacant by Mr Kennedy's going out to join the Free Church.

On one of his customary tours through the Parish of Kirkhill, Farquhar got a night's lodging at Inchberry, in a house or outhouse in the corner of which a pig happened also to be accommodated. Farquhar's bed appears to have been put rather close to where grumply was lying. Before morning it became restless and, with the curiosity of its kind, poked its snout into the other's face. *'Chan eil e na chleachdadh aig aon a bhith gam phògadh 's cha leig mi leat a dhèanamh an dara uair,'* ('No one is in the habit of kissing me and I won't allow you to do it a second time') cried Farquhar as he seized the pig by the hind legs and dashed its brains out against the wall, evidently angry at the indignity inflicted on him in putting him to sleep with such an animal.

Poor Farquhar lived to be over eighty years of age and almost to the last maintained wonderful vitality. When, however, the inevitable break came, a neighbour took pity on him and conveyed him to the Northern Infirmary where he died on 21st September 1868.[73]

Possessed of considerably greater mental powers was a famous Skye fool, who flourished in the early part of the nineteenth century, called *Gilleasbuig Aotrom*, or 'Light-headed Archie'. From the stories that have come down to us regarding him, one is doubtful whether he were not, in some respects, more rogue than fool. His wit was of the sharpest, his songs and epigrams most caustic. 'Archie, although a public beggar, possessed excellent manners,' says Dr Norman McLeod. 'He was welcomed in every house in Skye and, if the landlord had any appreciation of wit, he was sure to ask him into the dining room after dinner to enjoy his racy conversation. The fool was ready to engage in any war of joke or repartee and to sing some inimitable songs which hit off, with rare cleverness, the infirmities and frailties of the leading people of the Island, especially the clergy.'

In fact, some of the clergy and gentry were so much afraid of being made the subjects of his wit that they endeavoured, by generous largesse and hospitality, to keep on good terms with him. A Skye laird met him one day gnawing a bone. 'I think,' he said, 'it is time you got rid of that bone.' 'What will I do with it?' replied the fool. 'Give it to the first dog that meets you.' 'Here you are then,' said Archie, 'I don't believe I will meet a bigger dog than yourself for a day or two.'

Archie's practical jokes were as remarkable as his sayings. In his time there was a certain old minister in Dunvegan, called Mr Souter, who lived in fear of Archie's sharp tongue and upon whose weakness and good nature the latter readily preyed. One cold winter's night, when

---

73   For further stories of Farquhar and his famous prayer see *Fearchair-a-Ghunna* 1995.

everyone was snug in bed, a thundering knock at the door aroused the minister. Putting his head out of the window, he recognised Archie. 'Is this you, Archie? What, my good friend, do you want at this hour of the night?' 'What should a man want at this hour,' was the reply, 'but his supper and his bed?' Knowing with whom he had to deal and being afraid of him, the good man partially dressed himself, descended the stair, opened the door for the rogue and then searched the pantry until he had set a substantial supper before him. When Archie had satisfied himself with this, 'Now,' said Mr Souter, 'there is a fine warm bed in the stable loft where you will be most comfortable till morning.' 'Well,' said Archie, 'it has always been the custom of our country for a gentleman to show his guest to his bedchamber. Had you not better come with me yourself and light me to my "nice warm bed"?' 'O, I'll do that,' said the amiable minister. A ladder led up to the loft and Archie, with an appearance of being very polite, insisted that his host should ascend first. When the minister had entered the loft, Archie, who had stood meanwhile at the foot of the ladder, shouldered it, exclaiming: 'Well, if the bed is so very warm and comfortable, I wish you joy of it.'[74]

On another occasion, Archie happened to be down at the pier at Portree where some fishing boats were lying. Seizing a cod from one of the boats without the knowledge or during the absence of the crew, he set off up the town with it. He knocked at a certain door and when the good man himself opened it, he asked: 'Will you buy this fine big cod?' 'What is its price?' 'Only a shilling,' was the answer. 'O yes and thankful to get it,' said the man, producing his shilling. Archie, taking it from his hand, remarked that, as he was not busy that morning, he would just take the fish down to the burn and clean it, to which the buyer readily assented. Our friend then took the fish and, in the same manner, sold it with equal success at seven other houses. Then he took it back to the boat from which he had taken it, casting it among the others and exclaiming to the crew: '*Siud agaibh 'illean chòir bhur trosg 's ma phàigheas e sibh cho math 's a phàigh e mise, 's math an beathach e (e*

---

74 Retold from McLeod 1867, pp. 314–7. The further stories of Archie, including the poem concluding this chapter, do not appear in the 1867 edition. I must therefore assume the author had access to a fuller, probably Gaelic edition.

deagh iasg a th'ann).' ('There, my lads, is your cod and if it will pay you as well as it has done me, it is a good fish.')

On one of his wanderings, Archie came to a house in a glen in the back of the Island, where he was unknown. He knocked at the door and cried: 'Is anyone in?' 'Well,' replied a woman's voice, 'there are not many in but won't you come in yourself?' 'Is there no one in but yourself?' 'Yes,' was the answer, 'John is in, but he is in bed and has been for five years.' 'What's the matter with him?' 'I really don't know.' 'Well,' said Archie, 'he has been too long lying in that condition. I'm a doctor myself and perhaps I may be able to do something for him.' 'Thankful am I to see you,' said the poor woman. A pot was boiling on the fire and Archie asked her, after he had examined the sick man, what it contained. She told him it was a fowl she was boiling for her husband. 'A fowl?' exclaimed the assumed physician. 'That might prove fatal to him in his present condition. You had better give me the fowl and I will tell you afterwards what you are to do for your husband.' The simple woman took the fowl from the pot and set it before Archie, who leisurely made his dinner of it, while he cast sundry glances at the sick man in the bed.

'Now,' he said, when he was finished, 'I see you have a cow and a young calf at the other end of the house. You will just take hold of the calf and skin it. Then put the calf skin on your husband, place him under the cow and if she does not take to him, set the dogs at her and drive her up to the rocks.' The poor woman lifted up her two hands and rushed out of doors to seek help. She recognised at length that her visitor was deranged in mind but, before she returned, the 'doctor' had disappeared.

On one of his expeditions to the mainland, Archie happened on a certain Sunday to be in Glenshiel and, as his custom was, he went to church. Not content with taking a back seat he went boldly forward and sat down on the pulpit steps leaning, like Jacob of old, on the top of his staff. The minister, good man, seeing the stranger taking this unusual seat, imagined that he must be somewhat deaf. For a time all went well until some shepherds' dogs, that had accompanied their masters into church, began to move about and, as their manner is, to exhibit their common brotherhood by a low growling at each other. In a few minutes they would have settled down quietly again at their masters' feet had not Archie thought it an occasion for interference, with the inevitable result that growling grew to snarling and snarling to fighting, while Archie laid about him with his staff and the shepherds, in their excitement, whistled and cried to their dogs. In a pause of the turmoil the minister shouted to his elders: 'I wish you would put that poor man outside.' '*B'fhearr leam gun cuireadh sibh an duine truagh sin a mach as an eaglais,*' answered Archie. '*Cha ruig sibh a leas dragh chur oirbh fhein. Tha mise air a bhith fada gu leòr an seo, 's mas e bhur ceòl feadaireachd, tha pailteas suid gu leòr d'ur, searmoin dhomhsa – mòran ga ràdh ach beagan ga dheanamh latha math leibh.*' ('You need not trouble yourself, I have been long enough here and, if your music is whistling, I've had plenty of your sermon – plenty being said and little being done. Goodbye to you.')

In my own native Parish of Kenmore in Perthshire,[75] there still survives the memory of a famous fool, who lived and wandered in Glen Lyon and Strathtay during the first half of the nineteenth century. His name was Duncan MacGregor and he was born at Artrasgart in Glen Lyon, his father having a small-holding in that Glen. Duncan was often called 'Garth's Fool' because he received much kindness from Stewart of Garth and often paid long visits to Garth House, where he could always rely on getting 'a bite, sup and a bed'. He is, however, best remembered in his native district as '*Donnchadh Mòr na Pìoba*' (Big Duncan the Piper).

When Duncan was only a lad, his father died leaving his mother with the care of a twin sister and himself, both naturals, and two younger sons, both very bright boys. The young widow made a gallant fight for her children's welfare and, although terribly handicapped, she yet secured sympathy and kindly assistance and at length reaped the reward in seeing one of her sons a respected minister of the Church of Scotland and the other a parish schoolmaster.

Through the influence of the Menzies chief of the day, the boys, Robert and Alexander, who were the cleverest boys in the school, received, one after the other, the appointment of Parish Schoolmaster of Dull. From that the elder proceeded to college, became a licentiate of the Church and latterly Minister of Kilmuir in Skye.[76] When Robert

---

75 The Author's grandfather farmed at Boreland in the vicinity of Kearnan – see biographical details in the Introduction.

76 Robert's son was the Revd Alexander MacGregor, the greatly loved Minister of the West Church, Inverness, while the second brother's grandson – another Alexander – became a solicitor in Inverness.

was licensed and was to preach in the Parish Church of Dull, his sister Margaret was very anxious to hear him and pleaded with her mother and brother to let her go to church. On promising to keep quite still and silent, she was allowed to go. The sermons in those days were somewhat longer than they are wont to be today and, before the preacher concluded, Margaret, who had sat gazing in open-mouthed wonder at him, became more and more fidgety. At last, when he stopped, a voice was heard exclaiming: 'A *laochain, nach ann agad fhèin a tha'n gab.*' ('O laddie, what a gift o' the gab ye hae.')

It must have been some time after this that Robert was asked by the Revd Mr MacVean, the Minister of Kenmore, to preach for him. Duncan, who was very fond of attending church, of course made it a point to be present on the great day on which his honoured brother was to officiate. There he was, sitting in the front seat of the gallery, and when his brother entered the pulpit from the vestry Duncan looked round with an air of exaltation, as if to say, 'That is my brother.' It happened to be a warm summer day and the church was crowded to hear the young preacher, so the doors were left open. When Robert was about the middle of his discourse a turkey, belonging to the Kenmore innkeeper, with the boldness of his tribe stalked through the open door into the church and half-way up the passage. There he stood for a moment, lifted up his head toward the preacher and cried: 'Bul-ul-ul,' then turned and ran out with the beadle at his heels. The gravity of the congregation was naturally upset. Among others who had to hide their faces in their hands was the venerable minister, Mr MacVean, who was sitting in the Manse seat just under the pulpit. You can imagine Duncan's annoyance and indignation at what he regarded as an insult to his brother. He, however, said nothing.

Next Sabbath he was sitting in his former seat in the gallery. When Mr MacVean was just entering on the second head of his sermon Duncan rose, clattered down the gallery stair, strutted into the church with his hands beneath his coat-tails, walked up till he was just under the pulpit, lifted up his head towards the minister, as he had seen the turkey doing, and cried: 'Bul-ul-ul-ul!' He then stalked out again with the proud sense of having avenged an indignity.

Duncan, as I have mentioned, was called 'the Piper'. From his boyhood he was ambitious to be a piper and he somehow managed to get a set of bagpipes with which he went up and down the country. 'He played,' says Dr Duncan Campbell, in his *Reminiscences and Reflections of an Octogenarian Highlander*,[77] 'bits of laments and marches and reels all mixed up in comical disorder and disharmony. But he admired his own performances and this made him proud and happy, especially when, at weddings, he got a lot of the children to dance and shout around him as he played.' However, he expected a piper's welcome and fees wherever he went. Gentlemen gave him money, some of which he took home to his mother, some of which he hid in the woods, and I remember how, as boys, we used to search for some of Duncan's hoards. His dress, as might be expected, was somewhat peculiar. He wore on his head an old chimney-pot hat and often, for a kilt, a woman's petticoat with a kind of sporran. On his feet were brogues with hose or stockings as necessity decreed.

He was fond of wandering far afield and he somehow managed to find his way to Edinburgh to attend the Caledonian Gathering, there to exhibit his musical powers. It was there he became known as Garth's Fool, Garth being the well-known General Stewart, author of *The Highlanders of Scotland*, and prizes, in the shape of silver coins, were presented to him by some of the gentry who knew him. Duncan was not accustomed to pay for anything and usually, when he boarded the ferryboat at Burntisland, someone paid for him or else the ferryman let him cross without payment.

But on one occasion he found a new ferryman in charge, who demanded his fare and threatened to turn him off the boat unless he did so. Duncan jumped ashore and, turning to the ferryman, shouted in defiant tone: 'Tho' it's *leathann* it's no *domhainn*, she'll *togaidh* her *fèile* and go *troimhe*.' ('Tho' it's broad, it's not deep, she'll lift her kilt and go through'), at the same time, suiting the action to the word as he made his way down to the beach. Some of those on board, fearing that this mad fellow would try to carry out his purpose, called him to come back and that it would be all right. At the same time, they proffered his fare to the ferryman who, after that, allowed Duncan a free passage going and coming.

At one of these Gatherings he had somehow got inside the ring,

77 Campbell 1910.

where the pipers were competing, or about to compete. He was proceeding to tune up his pipes when one of the stewards, recognising him for what he was, rushed forward to him, crying: 'Stand back, man!' Duncan, giving a glance at the sheepskin under his arm, turned indignantly upon the steward: '*Cha do sgàin am baga, a dhuine!*' ('The bag has not burst, man!')

Some years after his minister brother had been settled in the Parish of Kilmuir in Skye, he and his family were seated round the study fire one wild winter night, listening to the snow being driven against the window, when suddenly the weird skirling of the bagpipes was heard. No tune could be distinguished, only an eerie reiteration of notes. All at once the minister started from his seat. 'If Duncan is alive,' he exclaimed, 'that is he; and if not, it is his ghost. Let us go out and see who it is.' So out they went in the direction of the sound and found Duncan lying helpless and almost benumbed behind a stone wall, where he had sunk down, exhausted after a terrible fight with the elements since leaving Portree. He would surely have perished from exposure had he not bethought him to try, by means of his pipes, to obtain succour, if such were to be near at hand. By the kindness of Providence he had been brought very near to his brother's manse. After he had been carried into the manse and warmed and had recovered his power of utterance, he remarked, as if apologising for his breakdown: '*Mur b'e a' ghaoth cha' tugainn baol air a chaitheamh.*' ('Were it not for the wind, I wouldn't care a jot for the drifting.')

In connection with every religious revival there are always a number of excitable individuals who, without waiting to acquire knowledge and spiritual experience, are over-fond of letting their own voices be heard. One such young man was once, with a great deal of gesticulation and much excited shouting, haranguing a little company in a Glen Lyon farmhouse at which Duncan happened to be present. Suddenly Duncan bent over to a deaf old woman, the mother of the speaker, who was sitting beside him and remarked in a whisper loud enough to be heard by all: '*Nach sinn bu chòir dhuinn a bhith taingeil gun do dh'fhàg Dia ar ciall againn.*' ('Should *we* not be thankful that God has left us our reason.')

At the General Election which followed the passing of the Reform Act, Lord Ormelie, son and heir of the Marquis of Breadalbane, was

Statue of Major General David Stewart of Garth at Keltneyburn.

brought forward to contest Perthshire in the Whig interest, and a meeting to promote his candidature was held in Fortingall, which all the local Whig gentlemen attended. Among those present was Campbell of Boreland who, not long before, had been tried for manslaughter. One night he had fired at a man who had broken into his house and who, when challenged, did not reply or stop. The man was badly wounded and later died of his injuries and Boreland was arrested, but was found not guilty at his trial.

At this Fortingall meeting, Duncan, who knew that where gentlemen assembled, especially at election time, he was likely to get some money, was present and in the pauses of the oratory he would interject some skirls of his pipes. At the close he went round, hat in hand, to receive his piper's fee and made a haul of sixpences and shillings. Boreland, having no smaller coin, threw in a half-crown into the hat. Duncan, who had probably never seen such a large silver coin before, lifted it out, gazed at it, inspected it on both sides and, finding it to be quite a sterling coin, looked up into Boreland's face in an ecstasy of gratitude, exclaiming: "*S math nach do chroch iad sibh.*' ('It is a good thing they did not hang *you*.')

Duncan was, like others of the same type, made use of by the small lairds of the district to carry messages and parcels, sometimes considerable distances. He was always willing, for a silver coin and a good dinner, to do this and almost invariably 'carried out his instructions with promptitude and fidelity'. General Stewart of Garth placed the utmost reliance upon his faithful discharge of any commission entrusted to him and boasted of this on one occasion to Sir Neil Menzies, a neighbouring laird. Sir Neil said he would put him to a test and see whether he was quite so reliable. 'I will give Duncan a basket,' he said, 'to carry to Garth House[78] and we will see whether he will deliver it as he got it.'

Duncan was asked to go to Castle Menzies. On his arrival there, he was taken to the kitchen and well fed; then Sir Neil gave him a basket, carefully tied along with a letter, both of which he was to deliver to

---

78   It is not clear, from the Author's account, whether these incidents took place at Garth House on the bank of the River Lyon or at Garth Castle, some two miles away on the Keltney Burn, as both names are used in the original manuscript.

General Stewart at Garth House. He was particularly enjoined not to open the basket. Duncan went on his way, but the day being hot he stopped to rest under the shade of some trees. He had been feeling curious as to what the basket contained and his curiosity was whetted when he began to feel movements inside it. He was in a quiet place where no one would see him, so he thought no harm could be done and no one would know if he unfastened the cord round the basket and peeped within. But he had scarcely touched the lid when it was thrust open from within and out leaped a hare, which disappeared in a moment among the bushes and bracken. Duncan closed the basket carefully again, hoping no one would be the wiser, and went on to Garth House. Going into the kitchen, he delivered both basket and letter to one of the maids. In a few minutes he was called up to the hall by the General, who stood with an open letter in his hand. Putting his finger upon it, he said: *'Tha maigheach an seo, a Dhonnchadh.'* ('There's a hare here, Duncan.') Before he could say more, Duncan, cutting a caper in huge delight, cried out: *"S math sin, shaoil leam (bha mi smaoineachadh) gun do chaill mi e.'* ('That's good, I thought I had lost it.')

Poor Duncan lived to be an old man, between seventy and eighty years of age. At last he was unable to move about, as he had been accustomed to do, and he was taken to the house of his brother, the schoolmaster, where he died. It was shortly before this that the Parish Minister of Fortingall came to see him and spoke earnestly to him of religious matters, especially about the afterlife. Poor Duncan did not seem to grasp, with much attention or concern, what was being said to him and he hearkened listlessly until the minister began to speak of the resurrection and the general rising again of the dead. All at once Duncan became alert and listened with open mouth and eyes. *'An èirich iad uile?'* (Will they all rise?) he at length exclaimed. *'Èirigh a h-uile duine,'* said the minister. ('Yes, every one.') *'Dilliman, Dilliman,'* he cried, with tears in his eyes and clapping his hands, *'chi mi an Seanailear, chi mi an Seanailear.'* ('I shall see the General again.') His excitement was so great at the thought of reunion with his old friend, hero and benefactor, General Stewart, who had died many years before at St Lucia in the West Indies, where he was Governor.

In that very interesting book of Highland reminiscences called *A*

Hundred Years in the Highlands, by Osgood Mackenzie[79] of Inverness, he tells of one Ian Bait from Loch Broom. He was accustomed to go about singing Gaelic songs at the top of his voice. On one occasion he fell into the Ullapool river when it was in flood and commenced yelling: '*Bàthadh! Bàthadh! A Dhè glèidh mise!*' ('Drowning! Drowning! O God, save me!') But soon he got managed to get hold of a bush on the bank of the river and felt himself in less danger, so he called out: '*Dh'fhaodadh ('S dòcha) nach ruig thu leas.*' ('O, perhaps you need not trouble.')

Like many another simple-minded fellow, Ian could also be mischievously ingenious at times. One night, after the Ullapool people had been annoying him, he revenged himself on them in the following manner. Seeing a long line, with hundreds of hooks baited with herring, lying in an outhouse ready to be set in the sea, he waited till everyone was in bed and then set it right along the village front. As Ullapool largely indulged in ducks in those days and as ducks, unlike hens, are night feeders, the long line was doing its dreadful work all night. Next morning, endless operations, many of which proved fatal, had to be performed by the angry householders.

Let me conclude with a tribute to the linguists of the Western Isles, educated and uneducated alike, from the lips of Archie, the 'fool of Skye'. Mr Souter, to whom we alluded earlier, was a good scholar in many languages but, unfortunately for his position in the Islands, not very expert in Gaelic. So Archie one day came up with the following rhyme:

> *Nuair thèid thu don chùbaid*
> *Ni thu urnuigh 'bhios gleusda*
> *Bidh cuid dhi na Gàidhlig*
> *Is pàirt dhi na Beurla*
> *Bidh cuid dhi na h'Eabhra*
> *Na Frangais 's na Greugais*
> *'S a chuid nach tuig cach dhi*
> *Bheir e gàir air fear Gheusda.*

> When you enter the pulpit
> Your prayer will be splendid

---

79 Mackenzie 1921.

Part of it will be Gaelic
And part of it English;
Part will be Hebrew
And some French and Greek
And what others will not understand
Will give a laugh to the Laird of Gesto.[80]

---

80 McLeod *Reminiscences*. Gesto is now a ruin, but is said to have been one of the oldest houses in Skye and owned outright by a cadet of the Mcleods of Dunvegan from the 15th century until forced into a leasing agreement with the Chief in 1674, probably as a result of a drinking bout leading to a duel or murder of a friend (see Otta F Swire *Skye* 1961, pp. 171–4).

Chapter 4

The Trail of the Fox

Of all the Highland chiefs of those stirring times in the history of the Highlands of Scotland, from the latter half of the seventeenth and the first half of the eighteenth centuries, none equals in interest, in intellectual ability and political dexterity Simon Fraser, Lord Lovat. The Frasers, like the Grants, are an old Norman family who managed, through marriage and forfeiture, to secure possession of a large heritage in the County of Inverness and to found a strong and numerous clan passionately devoted to their chiefs.

Their possessions consist of two parts, separated from each other by the Barony of Urquhart,[81] which belongs to the Grants. The one consists of Stratherrick, on the south-east side of Loch Ness – in the eighteenth century a wild, inaccessible, scarcely civilised district, a fit hiding place in times of danger, from whence one could, with a force of clansmen, make a sudden raid upon the low country about Inverness and, after burning or destroying, carry away booty of corn or cattle. The other section was the land along the south side of the Beauly Firth, from Inverness westward, penetrating along the Beauly River into the wilds of Strathglass and Strathfarrar. The land here is rich and productive and a number of families, cadets of the Lovat family, held land there under their chief in tack or warset. They were the gentlemen, the demie-wassals (*daomi-usish*) of the clan, owing fealty to the head of it, yet with a certain independence of spirit and position.

Simon was born probably in the year 1676. He was the second son of Thomas of Beaufort, who was grand-uncle of the then chief, Hugh, 11th Lord Lovat.[82] Simon's elder brother, Alexander, a very promising

---

81 Castle Urquhart, at the head of Glenurquhart, has an imposing view of Loch Ness and is one of the sites from which 'The Monster' is said to have been seen.

82 The succession given by James Fraser 1674 refers to him as 16th Lord Lovat. For a full history of the Lovat Frasers, from their 13th century origins to 1674, see William McKay's edition 1907 (reprinted 1974) of James Fraser's *Chronicles of the Frasers: The Wardlow Manuscript*.

lad, a graduate of Aberdeen University, led the Frasers at the battle of Killiecrankie, was severely wounded there and carried home in a litter to die. This death meant a great change in Simon's position and outlook and, apparently, awakened his slumbering ambitions or directed his thoughts into a new channel. He himself, after studying at the Grammar School in Inverness, proceeded to Aberdeen, where he graduated in 1695.

He was about to commence the study of civil law when he was offered a commission in a regiment, then in process of being raised by Lord John Murray, eldest son of the 1st Marquis of Atholl, for the service of King William. Apparently the offer was first made to Lord Lovat, who passed it on to his young kinsman, as offering a career to him. Simon, in his *Memoirs*, affirms that he at first refused it indignantly, because he was a Jacobite in sympathy, but that Lord Murray persuaded him to accept by saying that he was really raising the regiment to be used ultimately in the service of the exiled King James. At any rate, it is to be noted that Simon became an officer in the service of William of Orange and took the oath of allegiance to him.[83]

Hugh, Lord Lovat was a young nobleman of somewhat weak character and, Simon says, 'of contracted understanding'. He was married to Amelia, daughter of the Marquis of Atholl and by her he had four daughters, the sons, if any, having died in infancy. In his contract of marriage, dated 18th May, 1685, the estate was settled upon the male issue of the marriage, in default of whom 'to the heirs whomsoever of the marriage with a preference to the eldest daughter.'

It cannot be supposed that Simon would quietly acquiesce in this disposition, which deprived him both of the property and the chiefship to which, according to all Celtic rule and custom, he felt himself to be the rightful heir. Nor was it at all likely that a proud, warlike clan like the Frasers would view with favour their position under a woman, when such a vigorous personality as Simon's claimed their fealty. We may take it that the latter would endeavour to alter matters in his own favour.

In 1696, Lord Lovat went south to London to be presented to King

---

83 For the Murrays of Athole (Atholl) and their alliances with the royal houses of Europe, see Alan McNie *Clan Murray* 1988.

William and who more fitting to take with him, as henchman and companion, than young Beaufort, then a tall, handsome, powerfully built young Highlander. Evidently a gay time was spent in the metropolis and, as usual in those times, there was much drinking. Simon had a stronger head for this form of dissipation than many others; probably he restrained himself and watched his chance. At any rate, we find that in London Lord Lovat signed a new deed, annulling the former disposition of his estates and conveying them to Thomas Fraser of Beaufort, as male heir, in case he died without male issue and, on the same date, he executed a bond for 50,000 merks Scots in favour of his cousin, Simon Fraser, 'for the special love and affection' he bore to him. It is noted by Hill Burton that the above deed, although written by an English scrivener (Philip Dyer in St Martin's parish), is prepared in Scottish legal style, with the implication that Simon had got it drawn up in Edinburgh and carried it in his pocket, till he got his cousin, in a weak moment, to sign it.[84] Hugh, whose constitution was never strong and which had been weakened by the dissipation and fatigue of London, took ill on the way home and died in Perth.

When the new will was produced, the Atholl family, who had expected to be able to extend their powerful territorial influence over the Aird and who, at any rate, regarded themselves as the guardians of their sisters and their children's rights, were chagrined to find how matters stood. They probably felt that the Dowager Lady Lovat and her daughters had been robbed by Simon's cunning craftiness and Lord Tullibardine, the title to which Lord John Murray had been advanced, tried to get Simon to sign a renunciation of the estates by promising to secure a regiment for him, but Simon refused.

Shortly afterwards, he proceeded north to aid his father in getting possession of the estates, for the whole Atholl interest, which was very powerful in Scotland, was engaged in upholding the original disposition in favour of the late Lord's young daughter. Simon, in his determination to seize and hold the estate, was at once joined with a body of his

84   John Hill Burton, *Lives of Simon Lord Lovat and Duncan Forbes of Culloden*, 1847, p. 15. Moray McLaren, *Lord Lovat of the '45*, 1957, p. 29 assumes more kindly that the deed was 'drawn up in London under the eye of one familiar with Scottish law'. All agree, however, that they were probably genuine papers.

clansmen in the mountains but in the Low Country they were not so ready to come to his support. Indeed, a movement was initiated by some of them, at the instigation of Tullibardine, to invite Lord Saltoun and his heir to pay a visit to the Lovat country. Lord Saltoun was himself a Fraser, of a branch long settled in Aberdeenshire, and the evident intention of the invitation was to betroth the young heiress to the Master of Saltoun, as the Fraser Clan seemed determined to have a chief of their own name.

It may be asked, why not betroth her to Simon and thus overcome all disputes and difficulties? Although she was only ten or twelve, I do not suppose Simon would have objected to the betrothal, but for some reason the Atholl influence vetoed this. The Beauforts and their adherents were furious at the idea of an interloper like Saltoun coming among them and a protest, drawn up in all likelihood by Simon, was sent by sixty of the principal men of the Clan, hinting that he would repent it if he came.

Ignoring the threat, Saltoun, along with Lord Mungo Murray,[85] visited Lady Lovat at Castle Dounie[86] where she then resided, and matters went prosperously. After several days, Saltoun set off on his homeward journey with high hopes of seeing his son Lord Lovat. As they were passing through the wood at Bunchrew, they suddenly found themselves face to face with Simon and a number of followers, fully armed. Taken unawares, they were promptly seized and disarmed and then led back to the Castle of Fanellan, where they were incarcerated. A few days afterwards, a grim gallows was erected in front of the room in which Lord Saltoun was confined and he was told to prepare for being launched into Eternity; that he had but two days to live. The consequence of this threat was

---

85 2nd Viscount Stormont and younger brother of the Earl of Tullibardine (see *Clan Murray*, p. 28).

86 There is often confusion of the present Castle Beaufort, until very recently owned by the Lovat family, with Castle Dounie, referred to in the *Wardlaw Manuscript* at one point as 'the palace of Lovat'. It was almost certainly situated closer to the Beauly Firth, possibly in the district of Wester Lovat near Kirkhill. It was, of course, the family home at that time of Hugh, Thomas's grand-nephew and was razed to the ground in 1746, along with many other great family houses, as part of the aftermath of Culloden, by the forces of the Duke of Cumberland (see Prebble 1967, p. 166).

that he fell seriously ill. He begged for life and was granted it on condition that he would sign an undertaking to renounce all designs on the Estate. On giving this, he and the others with him were set free and escorted out of the Lovat bounds.[87]

Having committed this outrage, Simon proceeded to a still more violent and dastardly one. He seized Lady Lovat herself and kept her prisoner in her own castle and, in the words of a contemporary document, 'when nothing that she could propose or promise would satisfy them, the said Captain Simon Fraser and his complices made the Lady close prisoner in her chamber and then they come upon her with the said Mr Robert Munro, Minister at Abertarff,[88] and three or four ruffians about two or three in the morning and he proposes that she should marry him, and when she fell in lamenting and crying the great pipe was blown up to drown her cries and the villains ordered the Minister to proceed. And though she protested with tears and cries, nevertheless the said Minister proceeds and declares them married persons.'

Thus was consummated one of the strangest weddings in Scottish history and occasion given for the charge of rape which, at least in its lesser Scottish indictment of 'rapt',[89] was to taint Simon's reputation for the rest of his life. After this forced marriage, he kept her close confined on the Island of Aigas, and it is even said that the lady was at length brought to acquiesce in her position and got the Minister of Kilmorack to remarry them, as she was doubtful if the first ceremony was legal.

When Tullibardine heard of this outrage on his sister, he was naturally shocked and enraged. He immediately took proceedings in law against Simon and sent a force from Inverness to rescue her from his clutches.

---

87 Some part of this incident is said, by Hill Burton, to have taken place on Eileen Aigas, where the prisoners 'were kept in a "creel house", or cottage made with poles and wythes, a sort of wicker-ware cage, though the natural position of the island, set between fast flowing streams of the Beauly River, rendered further protection unnecessary.'

88 Not marked on modern OS maps, but an 1896 map shows the parish of Boleskine & Abertarff between Fort William and Fort Augustus. The River Tarff enters Loch Ness at Fort Augustus and the name is used frequently in the *Wardlaw Manuscript* for a hunting region at the head of the loch.

89 A crime said to be analogous to the mythical carrying off of Persephone, daughter of the Greek deities Zeus and Demeter, by Hades to be queen of the Underworld (Mackenzie 1934).

Simon had to flee and she was brought by her brother to Dunkeld. She never saw Simon again but she lived on until 1743.

Now the extraordinary thing is that although, in the correspondence of that time, both Simon and his father acknowledge the marriage and his father thinks they have gained a distinct advantage by this, yet afterwards Simon barefacedly denies the whole affair and marries two other ladies, as if his first wife were not in existence.[90] In his *Memoirs* he denies in the most lofty manner that he ever went near the Dowager Lady: 'The whole country knew that the Master of Lovat, at the age of twenty years, well educated, at the head of an ancient house might have aspired to any match in the Kingdom. He had no reason to commit the smallest violence upon a widow, who was old enough to be his mother' (she was only thirty-one), 'dwarfish in her person and deformed in her shape' – a wicked and probably unwarranted description.

In February 1698, a commission was delivered to Lieutenant Colonel Dalzell to search for and apprehend Thomas and Simon Fraser and their accomplices, as traitors and rebels, and bring them in, dead or alive. Simon sent his father to Dunvegan, the seat of MacLeod of MacLeod, whose sister he had married and there Thomas of Beaufort died in the following year. There may still be seen the monument erected by Simon to his memory, with its grandiose description as usual lauding Simon's own valour and virtues.[91]

On the heels of the Military Commission, proceedings commenced in the Court of Justiciary against them for high treason and for imprisoning and ravishing persons of distinguished ranks and continuing in arms after being charged to lay them down. Needless to say Simon did not appear to defend himself; he lurked among the fastnesses of Stratherrick and Strathglass and allowed himself to be condemned to be executed as a traitor. But it was evident he could not continue indefinitely secure, while defying the law of the land. So with commensurate

---

90 At least two other matrimonial excursions were attempted before this – in 1704 in Paris – with the apparent approval of the papal authorities (MacKenzie 1936, p. 75).

91 Boswell describes this 30 feet high pyramid, giving its inscription in full, in his *Journal* for 21st September 1773. Dr Johnson typically criticises the content as 'poor stuff, such as Lord Lovat's butler might have written'.

skill he made an appeal to the Duke of Argyll, in virtue of old marriage ties between the houses of Campbell and Fraser.

It was a well known fact that the Houses of Atholl and Argyll had long been rivals, sometimes deadly enemies, and this rivalry was by no means dead at that time, although for the moment they appeared on the same side of politics. Lovat suggested to Argyll that Atholl was becoming too powerful and self-aggrandising and ought to be checked, lest he should set the Highlands aflame. Argyll, suspicious of Atholl's proceedings and glad of an occasion to humble him, gave a ready ear to Lovat's appeal and urged Carstares, Principal of Edinburgh University and as Chaplain to William of Orange his most trusted confidante, that the King should be induced to pardon Simon for his convocation in arms while, as to the rest, he would stand his trial. On Argyll's recommendation he even ventured to go up to London to sue for pardon to King William. By the time he got there the King was in Holland, so Simon followed him to Loo[92] and through the influence of Carstares, got his pardon.

This was, of course, only in respect of the charge of treason. The other charges, of violence and rapt, still stood and he returned to Edinburgh, apparently prepared to face his trial. (In his *Memoirs*, written at a time when he wished to stand well with the Jacobites and to justify his appeal for pardon to William of Orange, he affirms that before going to Holland, he crossed to France to the Court of the exiled King James; that he was received cordially by the King, to whom he blackened the character of the House of Atholl, and that the King advised him for his Clan's sake to make peace with King William. But all this is scarcely credible.)

When he returned to Edinburgh, he at first took up a bold attitude of innocence and defiance of his accusers. When, however, he discovered that 'the wicked and abandoned judges', as he calls them, were determined on his condemnation, he fled again and so did not wait to receive the news of the dissolution of his sham marriage. A sentence of outlawry was pronounced against him for non-appearance. Yet we find Lovat after this, able to be in London evidently under Argyll's protection, and then

---

92 Now known as Het-Loo, near Apeldoorn; a royal palace was built here for William in 1686.

in his own country levying rent from the people, but always in danger of apprehension and summary execution.

When King William died and Anne acceded to the throne, Tullibardine became still more powerful and Lovat's own patron, Argyll, lost much of his influence. Simon, therefore, determined on a bold move. No prospect opened under the present regime of rehabilitating himself and recovering his estates. So he resolved to take steps toward the restoration of the exiled Stuarts, in the hope that, by these means, his own fortunes would be restored and honours would come to him. Before leaving the Highlands, he tells that he sounded some of the chiefs on their readiness to take up arms for the King over the Water. He even says that he induced a great number of the Lowland Lords to give him a commission to go to St Germain,[93] containing the same assurance. At any rate, in the autumn of 1702 we find him at the Court of Mary of Modena, the Queen Mother.[94]

At that shadow of a court, the centre of ceaseless intrigue, there was keen rivalry between the Duke of Perth, the Governor of the young King,[95] and Lord Middleton, the Secretary of State. Lovat attached himself, through his cousin Sir John MacLean of Duart, to Perth and shortly afterwards we find him becoming a convert to the Roman Catholic faith. This was evidently done for the purpose of ingratiating himself with the Queen Mother and with the Papal Nuncio, Gualterio, and through him being able to get the ear of Louis XIV of France for his projects. Middleton, from the first, was suspicious of him and very sceptical of his designs, for his own hopes of the restoration of the young James to the throne of his fathers were based on securing the adhesion of the English Lords, and it is fairly evident that Queen Anne herself was secretly favourable to her brother's succession. Middleton, therefore, deprecated any rash expeditions that might alienate the people of England and, particularly, any invasion of wild Highlanders, however loyal and brave and ardent they might be. On the other hand, Lovat believed that the restoration of the Stuarts would be deferred till

---

93 St Germain-en-Laye, 7 miles north of Versailles, was at this time the seat of the Court of the exiled King James.

94 Widow of James II of England, who had died in exile in 1701.

95 James Edward Stuart was then only 14.

Domesday if they waited for England to move. His plan was that of a rising in the Highlands and the seizure of Fort William by means of a French force.

Lovat's hopes, therefore, lay not so much at St Germain as at Versailles and he succeeded in obtaining an audience of Louis XIV, to whom he presented his scheme. When asked how many men could be raised in the Highlands, he named 10,000 – admitting later to his friend, Sir John MacLean, that it was an exaggerated number, put forward in order to persuade the King to take him seriously.

Louis was more willing to listen than Middleton, not because he was eager to help the Exiles but because, in the waning military fortunes of the moment with France near exhaustion in the war, a diversion in Scotland would, as in olden days, weaken England. That was the old policy of France and the secret of the 'Auld Alliance' between her and Scotland. While Louis listened with a measure of approval, he was persuaded by Middleton that it was advisable, before embarking on any such undertaking, to send Lovat back to Scotland to obtain more definite assurances of assistance. To this Lovat assented and he returned with a Captain John Murray, an officer in the French Army, who was instructed to repair straight to the Highlands, there to be introduced by Lord Lovat to the chiefs of clans and gentlemen of interest, from whom he was to inform himself 'what they propose, what they are able to do, what time they can be ready.'

Among the first whom Lovat visited in Scotland were the Duke of Argyll and Lord Leven, strange associates for a Jacobite emissary as they were among the chiefs of the Whig or Hanoverian side. To them he conveyed a desire to meet Lord Queensberry, the Queen's High Commissioner, as he had information to give. An interview having been accorded, Lovat told him how he had come from St Germain and mentioned certain letters that had been sent from there to the Duke of Hamilton, the Duke of Gordon and to Lord Atholl. The two former had been delivered, he said, but he had managed to get possession of the one to Atholl and he showed it. The only indication of the name of the person for whom it was intended were the letters 'L.M-y' on the outside. As these were written by another hand than that which wrote the rest, it is most probable, as Bishop Burnet conjectures, that it was Lovat himself who addressed it and that the whole intention of the

Queensberry Plot, as it became known, was to ruin his enemy Atholl, while at the same time helping himself and his cause by playing the role of double agent.

Queensberry reported to Queen Anne his intercourse with Lovat, although not mentioning his name, but he kept this secret from other members of the Government, of whom Atholl was one. When, at last, the whole story became known, many imagined that it was Queensberry's own plot to ruin a rival.

Lovat, meanwhile, had visited the Highlands and received promises of support from some of the chiefs, but others were lukewarm and hesitating and, besides, had no trust in the envoy himself. A meeting of Jacobite nobles was held at Drummond Castle, but it was neither representative nor enthusiastic, and a great difficulty cropped up as to who was to be the leader. After this, Lovat again saw Queensberry, got a pass to London and from London into Holland, and so was able to make his way back, through the lines of the opposing armies, to St Germain.

While in London, he had come in contact with Robert Ferguson, the Plotter, who had managed to obtain information out of him with regard to his dealings with Queensberry. Ferguson immediately conveyed the information to Atholl who, in great indignation, took steps to vindicate himself to Queen Anne. Friends and associates of Atholl were seized and, to save their lives, gave information and for the moment there was great excitement – a crisis in the political world.[96]

All this came to the ears of Middleton through his spies and so Simon, soon after he arrived at St Germain, found that his intrigues were known and his attempts to justify himself were not very successful. 'It is clear as daylight,' writes Middleton to De Torcy, Louis' Secretary for Foreign Affairs, 'that these noblemen [Queensberry, Argyll and Leven] wanted

---

96 In answer to the charge of trafficking with the enemy, William Burns in the *Inverness Courier*, 1907, claims it was an act of legitimate self defence by an officer of the Court of St Germain and that no person was 'implicated or punished by the Government from what Simon said.' It did, as intended, lead to a violent quarrel between Queensberry and Atholl, which led eventually to Queensberry's own fall from grace, and was undoubtedly a key factor in achieving the very opposite of what Lovat was fighting for – the Act of Union of Parliaments of England and Scotland in 1707 (see McLaren pp. 92–4).

to employ him as a spy and for signing letters and commissions that might serve as proofs against men of honour in that country [i.e. Scotland]. If the King thinks proper to apprehend him, it should be done without noise. His name should not be mentioned any more and, at the same time, all his papers should be seized.'

When Lovat realised how matters stood and the danger that threatened him, he wrote one of his humble, appealing letters to Middleton, enlarging upon his own services and sacrifices and those of his family and then promised to meddle no more with affairs until the King came of age. However, De Torcy acted on Middleton's suggestion but, instead of sending him by *lettre de cachet* to the Bastille, to which troublesome people were quietly consigned, he was simply exiled to Bourges, about 150 miles south of Paris. Louis, feeling he might yet be useful, allowed him a pension of a hundred crowns a month; but Lovat was always extravagant, always short of money and this tended to make him unscrupulous in the means he took to obtain it.

After some months of comparative freedom at Bourges, where he was able, among other diversions, to take a prominent role in arranging a fête to celebrate the birthday of the Duc de Bretagne, he was summarily transferred and imprisoned in the castle of Angoulême, thrust into a horrible dungeon where he remained in darkness for thirty five days. After this his treatment was mitigated. He became a prisoner on parole, first for three years at Angoulême and then at Saumur. At Saumur his circumstances were fairly comfortable, although doubtless very restrictive to his restless Highland spirit. There, however, he remained for eight years in receipt of a pension of 4,000 francs from Versailles.

It was there he made the acquaintance of distant kinsfolk: the Marquis and Marchioness de la Frezelière, head of a branch of the Fraser family that had remained in Normandy at the time of the Conquest. They were very kind to him and helped to make his life tolerable, if not pleasant.[97] He also became very friendly with the Jesuits, with whom he seemed to find much common ground and spent many hours in

---

97 The Marquis died in 1711, but from the lengthy correspondence of the Marquise it appears, not only that he had 'bequeathed him as a mark of affection his daughter in marriage' when she was old enough, but that he had already left behind him in France a natural child – '*très blond et de votre air*' (see MacKenzie 1936 and McLaren 1957).

theological discussion. It is this period which seems to have confirmed his claim, only made openly in his final days, of adherence to the Catholic faith. It is, however, not surprising that in such a situation, whatever devotion Lovat cherished to the Jacobite cause became very cold and that, when his ingenious schemes and plans went so far agley, he should meditate abandoning them altogether.

A letter in which he sought to ingratiate himself by doing service to the other side, was sent by him to Lord Leven. In it he spoke of an expedition being in preparation, of which he promised to give further information. Unfortunately for Lovat, Leven himself had turned a political somersault and was now favourable to the claims of King James (the Pretender). His letter was thus sent directly to Middleton, damaging his reputation irretrievably at the Jacobite court, now moved from St Germain to Bar-le-Duc, some 130 miles east of Paris.

To stem the tide of suspicion, Lovat sought the support of his old friend Gualterio, the Papal Nuncio. He begged him to obtain for him one of three favours: (1) a reconciliation with James and the Queen Mother; (2) permission to enter the service of France or (3) permission to leave the country. His appeal, however, was of no avail and he was forced to remain where he was.

It was during these years that the union of the Parliaments of England and Scotland was hurriedly effected against the wishes of a great many Scotsmen, who felt that Scottish interests had been betrayed. This made it all the more likely that, whenever Anne should die, a determined attempt would be made to overthrow the Hanoverian succession and restore James to his father's throne.

The Lovat estates were at this time held by the daughter of Hugh, Lord Lovat, the younger Amelia or rather by her husband, Alexander MacKenzie, a son of Lord Prestonhall, one of the Judges of the Court of Session and a brother of the Earl of Cromartie. In an apparent attempt to satisfy the demands of the original settlement, he had taken for himself the fanciful title of MacKenzie of Fraserdale. But as there had always been clan rivalry between the MacKenzies and the Frasers, and as the gentlemen of the latter clan discerned an attempt to abolish their own chiefship and make them, like the Macraes, vassals of the Mac-Kenzies, they pined for the return of him they all regarded as their chief.

They hoped that through the troubles that were almost sure to arise in the near future, 'something would turn up' both to their and his advantage. They felt that his appearance, with the clan at his back, would be decisive one way or another and I think, from the names of those foremost in the steps taken, that they hoped he would be found on the Anti-Jacobite side. A meeting of gentlemen of the clan was held and it was resolved to send one of them to France to search for Lovat and, if possible, bring him home.

The choice fell upon Major James Fraser of Castle Leathair (Castle Heather), a brother of Fraser of Culduthel and, although he protested that he knew no French and had a wife and eleven children, yet his friends evidently felt he was the one most likely to succeed. Travelling by way of London, Paris, Versailles, St Germain, Bar-le-Duc and Lunéville, the Major had many adventures where, in spite of the great language handicap, his pawkiness and mother wit joined to courage and readiness of resource stood him in good stead; and eventually he found his way to Saumur. Joyfully he was welcomed and the two clansmen began to concoct a means of escape. Taking French-leave of Saumur, they made their way to Rouen, thence via Dieppe to Boulogne, where they hired an open boat to convey them to Dover in November, 1714. From Dover they went to London.

Realising that it was possible to hide safely here when they could not do so elsewhere, the Major approached the Earl of Islay, a brother of the Duke of Argyll, on Lovat's behalf, and he also asked his old friends, Brigadier Grant (a brother of Sir Ludovic Grant of Grant) and John Forbes of Culloden, to speak on his behalf to Islay and Argyll. Islay was favourable but cautious and he gave the Major a petition in favour of Simon, to be signed by the leading gentlemen of the five Northern Counties, and told him to go north to obtain the signatures.

North the Major went in the dead of a stormy winter; travelled through the shires of Inverness, Moray and Nairn, getting the signatures of some by pretending it was to be presented to James VIII,[98] of others that it was intended for George I.[99] All this time Lovat was in hiding in London,

---

98 James Edward Stuart, son of the deposed James II of England (James VII of Scotland) and known in England as the Old Pretender.

99 George of Hanover was invited to become King of Great Britain on the death of Anne in 1714, as being the nearest Protestant heir, in accordance with British parliamentary acts of 1689 and 1701.

for Atholl and MacKenzie of Fraserdale had heard of his reappearance and a warrant for his arrest had been issued. No sooner had the Major returned from his drumming mission to the Highlands than the long arm of the Law caught up with the Fraser party in Soho Square at three in the morning of 11th June, 1715.

Meanwhile, among those displaced from office at the accession of George I had been the Earl of Mar, who promptly showed his resentment by becoming an active adherent of the Stuarts. He proceeded to concert measures for an attempt to restore the exiled dynasty and arrangements were made to time the rising for August, 1715. Previous to that a great hunting was arranged at Mar Lodge, to which came the Jacobite nobles and chiefs, and on 6th September the Standard of James was unfurled at Braemar.

When Lovat heard of this he felt that his hour of opportunity had come and must be promptly seized. He wrote what the Major calls a creeping letter to the Earl of Sutherland, the chief tower of strength to the Government in the North, promising his aid to the Government if he were liberated. Spurred on by the political uncertainties of the moment, Argyll and Islay were persuaded of Lovat's importance to the control of the Highland clansmen and, supported by Sutherland, managed to galvanise Government action in his favour. A bond for £5,000 as bail was found by the Earl and his friends and a pass was procured from Lord Townshend, the Secretary of State, in favour of the Major, Simon's brother John, and two servants. One of the servants was Simon himself. In great secrecy, but with a number of near-arrests, they made their way to Stirling, where Argyll was with the royal army, making ready to meet Mar and his Jacobite forces.

Lovat instructed the Major to request Brigadier Grant to tell Argyll that he was on his way north to create a diversion. Argyll asked the Major if he could trust Lovat. 'Be in no concern about him,' was the reply. 'If he offers to join the rebels, his head will be sent to Stirling.' The Duke was apparently satisfied and wished him 'God speed!' With John Forbes and the Major, they embarked on a vessel at Leith, which carried them to Fraserburgh. Here they had further close shaves with Jacobite forces, including a group led by Lord Saltoun of the Bunchrew Wood incident, but managed to complete their journey westward to Culloden House.

The Frasers had been led out by MacKenzie of Fraserdale to join Mar but at Culloden he heard that three hundred Stratherrick men had refused to follow him. So the next day, he sent the Major to Stratherrick to bring these men to their true Chief's side at Culloden and, on the following day, they were there, overjoyed to see and serve him. Inverness was then held by Sir John MacKenzie of Coul with three hundred men for James. With Lovat's coming, new energy was infused into the Whig or Hanoverian side. He drove back MacDonald of Keppoch who, with three hundred men, was coming to reinforce the garrison and immediately began to press in upon the town, so that within a few days the Governor and his forces were compelled to abandon the town and retire across the Firth to Rossshire.

The capture of Inverness was, indeed, an important stroke for, at a critical moment in the rising, it struck a serious blow at a vital spot, it checked and blocked the movement of reinforcements from the West and most of the North. Lovat also, by withdrawing the Frasers from Mar's standard, brought them bodily over to the other side. 'I find,' writes Argyll to Lord Townshend, 'Lord Lovat's being in the North has been of infinite service to His Majesty.' By his vigorous aid, the backbone of the rebellion was speedily broken in the North.

One can only speculate what the issue might have been, had he thrown his influence on the other side. What is very plain is that he put an effective spoke in the wheel of the Rebellion that prevented all possibility of success. Whatever his private predilections – one could not call them principles – he was well satisfied with himself, as well he might be for he had played a master stroke in his own reinstatement. The result of these valuable services rendered by him to the Government was a complete change in his fortunes and, through the error Fraserdale had made in joining Mar, he was able to take quiet possession of his own Castle Dounie. His pardon, which had been delayed, was at length granted. Not only so, but he was invited to London and had an interview of King George, who received him graciously and thanked him for his services. He also received a commission, appointing him Governor of the Castle of Inverness and Captain of an Independent Company of foot, with corresponding pay.

He himself had suggested, as an effective means for quelling the rebellious spirit among the Jacobite clans and disarming them, that five companies of 300 men each should be raised from the loyal clans and used as a kind of police along with regular troops, or where regular troops would be of little use (the same policy used in the present century on the Indian Frontier). The Government acted upon Lovat's suggestion and his own appointment to his Company was among the first to be made.[100]

He was very proud of his Company and held reviews of it on several occasions for the benefit of the citizens of Inverness and of his own vanity. He made it very efficient and passed most of his own clansmen through it, so as to make them formidable in arms and useful to himself in certain eventualities. These Independent Companies were afterwards re-modelled and Lovat, to his great chagrin, lost his command. They received a distinctive tartan of their own of a darkish colour and became known as the Black Watch. They were formed into a regiment and, contrary to their original design and purpose, were taken from the Highlands to London, on pretence of being reviewed by the King, and then shipped to Flanders. But originally, as you can see, they were raised for service in the Highlands.

When in London in 1716, Lovat also got a grant of the escheat[101] of the life-rent of the Lovat Estates, which was heavily bonded, in place of Fraserdale; about £300 per annum. He was back in London in 1717 and a newsletter of 4th November of that year has the following: 'The Duke of Atholl has received no marks of favour at Court but Lord Lovat has very great ones; a pension of £500, constant admission to the King, in spite of the Duke of Roxburgh and others, and one of the most frequent guests at the Royal Table, to the great mortification of the Duke of Atholl.' (It is scarcely doubtful, I think, who was the author of this paragraph. Simon was ahead of his time in making use of the Press and in perceiving the value of advertisement, particularly self-advertisement.) The tables were indeed turned on his old enemy, for Atholl was no longer in favour and with some reason, for his two sons, Tullibardine

---

100 It was also a remark of Lovat's, in a memorial to George I (1724), which probably led directly to General Wade's commission 'to inspect the situation of the Highlanders ... and suggest remedies'. The military roads of 1732 onwards were the result of that inspection. (See pp. 27–8 and Taylor p 18–19).
101 Handing over of property to which the legal title has lapsed by intestacy or forfeiture.

and Lord George Murray – the heroes of the '45 – had already joined the standard of the Stuart King, James.

Frequent visits to the South, to Edinburgh and London, by Lord Lovat are mentioned from this time for he became involved in a very torrent of litigation that lasted more or less all of his life. In fact, he had sometimes five lawsuits going on at the same time. He had to fight for his own right to the Estate as a male fief and for the overturning of the decision of the Court of Session in 1702, investing the daughter of the former Lord Lovat (Fraserdale's wife) with the Barony of Lovat. This was only decided in his favour in 1734.

There were also creditors of the Estate and creditors of his own of various kinds that instituted actions against him. Innumerable letters had to be written, lawyers primed with facts and arguments, judges to be approached, emplenished and wheedled, and wheels to be turned within wheels; all giving scope to Lovat's peculiar ingenuity and intellectual capacities. The intricacies of litigation gave singular scope to his type of mind and character and, while law was troublesome and expensive, he yet revelled in it. Poorer persons were afraid to enter into any legal dispute with him, knowing his skill, his unscrupulousness, his influence and the partiality of the judges he boasted he could count on.

For example, the Presbytery of Inverness and the Minister of Kirkhill allowed him to seize part of the glebe at Kirkhill rather than fight the case. One of his particular friends, or cronies, among the judges was James Erskine, a brother of the Earl of Mar, who fought at Sheriffmuir. He was raised to the bench as Lord Grange and was regarded as one of the pillars of the stricter Presbyterian party and an eminent example of piety. Dr Carlyle of Inveresk, however, tells how as a young man he met Grange and Lovat one day in Prestonpans and they took him to dine with them in an inn. The two Lords, then oldish men, drank deeply, then insisted on the landlady's buxom daughter coming in and dancing a reel, and gave 'such advices as men in a state of ebriety could give'.

When Grange wanted to rid himself of his termagant[102] wife, it was by Lovat's aid that he got her quietly removed from Edinburgh to the West Highlands, thence to be conveyed to lonely St Kilda, which belonged to his cousin, MacLeod of MacLeod. Here the poor dissipated,

---

102 A brawling overbearing woman.

half-mad woman lived for years and became wholly deranged – and little wonder![103] As readers of Scott know, that was an age of deep drinking, when the wisest and most eminent lawyers and statesmen spent their evenings over their wine until none was sober. It astonishes us today to read of men, not just like Grange or Lovat, but like Duncan Forbes of Culloden, the shrewd, prudent President of the Court of Session, indulging to such an extent in these intemperate convivialities. In fact, among the roisterers, Lovat was comparatively sober; he always kept his head and was able to make use of his weaker brother.

When matters had settled after the '15, and he had got quiet possession of his own domain, Lovat was anxious to get married. It was not a question of love with him but of policy, of strengthening his own position. He broached the business to his friends Argyll and Islay, while he intimated gently and plausibly that he was anxious to secure for them a stronger interest and influence in the North. The lady on whom he turned his favourable eye was Margaret, sister of Brigadier Grant of Grant, Argyll's friend and second in command, and knowing his own dubious record and reputation, he wanted them to further his suit. Islay was in some doubt about the risk of a 'pursuit of adherence by the other person' (the Dowager Lady Lovat, who lived until 1743) but Simon reassured him with the conviction that the lady denied the marriage in court and besides, that the minister and witnesses were all dead.

So, these objections and doubts being removed, his suit prospered, the lady and her friends consented, and Simon obtained an alliance with one of the most important and influential families in the North and one with a good record. Although the bride's father had died shortly before, the marriage was celebrated with great festivities that were long remembered in Strathspey. The marriage accounts tell of a half-hogshead of wine at £7 10s. Sterling, of 17 bolls of malt and 11 bolls for brewing Aqua Vitae (*uisge beatha* or whisky) and £385 Scots was sent to Aberdeen to buy the bride's trousseau.

---

103 St Kilda lies some 110 miles out into the Atlantic and its main island of Hirta was populated until 1930, when the islanders were evacuated at their own request. The Islands were bequeathed to the National Trust for Scotland in 1957 and declared Scotland's first World Heritage Site by UNESCO. The story of Lady Grange's ordeal was told in the style of a historical novel by W. C. MacKenzie: *The Lady of Hirta*, 1905 (See also Swire 1961, pp. 100–1).

As far as we can learn, the marriage turned out well; two sons were born and when shortly after the birth of the second in 1729, Lady Lovat died, he wrote to her brother: 'The Universe could not produce a better wife for my circumstances and temper; the most affectionate and careful wife that ever was born, whose chief care and greatest happiness was to please me in everything.'

Two years afterwards, we find him writing from Edinburgh to Fraser of Belladrum, commiserating with him on his bad health and, at the same time, intimating that the Laird of Luss had proposed a marriage for him with Sir Robert Dalrymple's daughter, Lady Luss's niece. He asks Belladrum to send south to him the rings and jewels that belonged to his deceased wife, adding 'that all that may save me money here'. The lady, however, was not enamoured of his courtship, in spite of the rings and jewels, and notwithstanding the pressure brought to bear on her by her family, she positively refused to marry him. At this he was both astonished and indignant, characterising her treatment of him as 'an indignity put upon his person and family that I can hardly bear'.

However, he soon found what he considered a more desirable match in Primrose Campbell, daughter of Campbell of Mamore, second son of the Duke of Argyll. She was only 23 and he was 57, so it is not altogether surprising that the marriage was not a success and after five stormy years they agreed to a separation. Lovat spoke of her as a mixture of 'a devil and a daw', probably because sometimes, 'even a worm will turn'. If there is truth in what Sir Walter Scott heard, that she was sometimes shut into her room 'a naked and half-starved prisoner', I suppose because she had not risen to his ideal of 'pleasing him in everything', then separation was best. Accusations of coarseness and bad temper were made against her, but she lived on in her flat in Blackfriars Wynd, off the High Street in Edinburgh – its aristocratic quarter then – on her small jointure till 1796, when she died at the age of 86. She was loved and honoured by all for her kindness and gentleness. It is said that 'as her chair emerged from the head of Blackfriars Wynd, anyone who saw her sitting in it so neat and fresh and clean would have taken her for a queen in waxwork, pasted up in a glass case.'[104]

There can be no doubt, I think, that on the whole Lovat was well-liked

---

104 Chambers *Traditions of Edinburgh* 1825.

by his own people. He regarded them as his own family and, so long as they did not quarrel with him, he was a considerate landlord and chief. For he was always to them the patriarchal chief who loved to have a numerous clan about him and to feel that he had authority over them as judge as well as laird, and that their chief end should be to serve and honour him. Should any of them try to oppose him, they at once became (in his favourite terms) unnatural and ungrateful villains.

His relations with the poorest of his people were marked by kindness and consideration. Generally he had a bag of farthings when he walked abroad, the contents of which he distributed among any beggars he met. He would stop a man on the road, inquire how many children he had, offer him sound advice and promise to redress any grievances he had. He would pat a boy on the head and if his name was Simon Fraser, give him half a crown. He would chat with an old woman, ask about her ailments and supply her on parting with snuff from his mull.[105] He was always ready with a joke here, a word of sympathy there, for did he not pride himself on being the father of his people? 'Were Gaelic wit and humour translatiable,' writes Mrs Grant of Laggan, 'the good things said by or to Lovat would furnish a jest-book.'

In 1718, when very ill in London, he indited a letter to his clan, of which the following is part: 'My dear friends, since by all appearance this is the last time of my life I shall have occasion to write to you ... I do declare before God ... that I loved you all: I mean you and all the rest of my kindred and family who are for the standing of their chief and name ... and God, to whom I must answer, knows that my greatest desire and the greatest happiness I proposed to myself under heaven was to make you all happy ... and that it was my constant principle to think myself happier with a hundred pounds and see you all live at your ease about me than have ten thousand a year and see you in want and misery. I did likewise design my poor commons to live at their ease, and have them always well-clothed and well armed after the Highland manner and not to suffer them to wear low-country clothes but make them live like their forefathers with the use of their arms, that they might always be in a condition to defend them against their enemies and do service

---

105 A snuff box, originally with a grinder; hence a mill or mull.

Wardlaw Mausoleum of the Lovat family at Kirkhill, built by Lord Hugh Fraser of Lovat in 1634 and heightened in 1722 by Simon to incorporate a fine pedimented memorial altar with the inscribed tablet commemorating his father (see text).

to their friends.'[106] This letter was to be kept in a box at Beaufort or Moniack and read once a year to the assembled clansmen.

In this connection and as characteristic of him, I give here the inscription he caused to be put on a monument erected within the family chapel at Kirkhill[107] to his father.

To the memory of Lord Thomas Fraser of Lovat, who chose rather to undergo the greatest hardships of fortune than to part with the ancient honours of his House and bore those hardships with undaunted fortitude of mind, this monument was erected by Simon Lord Fraser of Lovat his Son who likewise having undergone many and great vicissitudes of good and bad fortune through the malice of his enemies, He in the end at the head of his clan forced his way to his paternal inheritance with his sword in his hand and relieved his kindred and followers from oppression and

106 Mrs Thompson *Memoirs of the Jacobites of 1715 and 1745*, Vol III Appendix (c1845).
107 The Author was Minister of Kirkhill, 1908–12.

slavery; and both at home and in foreign countries by his eminent actions in the war and the state he has acquired great honours and reputation.

This inscription is clearly more to the honour of him who wrote it than to his father, and is a fair example of Simon's grandiloquence and vanity. Lest another might not be capable of writing a funeral inscription suitable to his own coffin, he prepared it himself and the plate which was to be put on that coffin still lies in the vault at Kirkhill. However, 'the best laid schemes of mice and men gang aft agley', for Simon's body lies far from there. The inscription is in Latin, of which the following is a translation:

> In this leaden sarcophagus are placed the remains of Simon Lord Fraser of Lovat who after twenty years in his own country and abroad with the highest praise and glory and perils of his life from the tyranny of Atholl and the wiles and plots of the Mackenzies of Tarbat restored and preserved his race and clan and family.
>
> Is it not the highest praise to preserve an ancient house? There is no honour to the enemy who has despoiled it. Although by the tricks and the stress of war he was strong, Simon by his wisdom and skill in war drove him out.

At his castle Simon kept a kind of court or levee, which a number of his retainers attended daily. One Donald MacLeod, an ex-sergeant of the Royal Scots, gives a vivid description of a dinner there. There was abundance of meat and drink. At the head of the table sat Simon and nearest him were the principal guests, neighbouring lairds or distin-guished strangers, who were regaled with French cookery and, for drink, claret or even champagne. Next to them were gentlemen of the clan, who enjoyed beef and mutton and to whom Simon would say: 'Cousin, I told my pantry lads to hand you claret, but they tell me you like port and punch best.' At the foot of the room would crowd the commoners of the clan, who got such viands as sheep's head and ale or whisky to drink. Outside was a crowd of domestics with little or no wages, herding on straw and snatching from the table the plates ere the guests were finished, in order to feed themselves.

Writing from Edinburgh to his second son, Alexander's tutor, left in charge of the house, he bids him 'to spare the hens rather than the mutton, to have two substantial dishes for dinner and three when there are strangers; to drink as much of the fine ale [Burn's 'tupenny'] as he has a mind, and when an extraordinary guest comes to give him a bottle of wine.'

It might have been supposed that, having secured his patrimony and having attained a long coveted position of importance in the Highlands, Lovat would have settled down as a peaceful and loyal, if not zealous subject of King George. But the temper of intrigue, chicanery and double-dealing was too deeply implanted in him. He was too restless, cunning and ambitious; too fond of fishing in muddy waters; too addicted to political intrigue and Macchiavellian methods, and too much self-deluded by his own dexterity to lead a quiet and straight life. He was extraordinarily vain and ambitious to make himself 'the greatest Lord Lovat that ever was', and although he had fought on the Government side in 1715, he could not rid himself of the old instinct of loyalty to the Stuarts. It smouldered on and with it the hope that the King would come to his own again and coming, would exalt him to very high rank of authority.

That, however, did not prevent him from taking a government pension and drilling his company for King George, perhaps with the hope that it might be useful on the other side. In 1721 a pardon was granted by James to Lovat, 'on his returning to [his] duty', which indicates that letters had passed between them. Two years later, Lovat was appointed by James as Lord Lieutenant of Inverness, Nairn and Sutherland and was ordered to seize Inverness and become its Governor. But Simon was already Governor of Inverness for King George and for the next twenty years represented himself to be both Whig and Protestant, a loyal servant of the Government. In 1733 he induced Sir James Grant to relinquish the Sheriffship of Inverness in his favour, and an excellent sheriff he made, keeping the County quiet and orderly and repressing all disorder with a strong hand by means of the companies under his command.

But from about 1730 onward rumours began to be spread abroad of his disaffection and of a new Jacobite movement, in which he was taking a leading part. He protests most vigorously against these calumnies of his enemies. 'I bless God,' he says, 'I never was in my life guilty of a base or villainous action, so I do not fear this wicked calumny.'

In 1736 Colonel John Roy Stuart of Kincardine, celebrated equally as Gaelic poet, doughty warrior and Jacobite enthusiast, was caught and imprisoned in Inverness gaol as a Jacobite emissary, stirring up rebellion. But he soon made his escape. Lovat was Sheriff at the time and it was alleged that he had given shelter to him at Dounie for six weeks after his escape, and that he sent a message to James by him. A witness afterward asserted that he heard Lovat asking Stuart to urge James to expedite his commission as Lieutenant-General of the Highlands and his patent as a duke. In 1739 he joined or founded a Jacobite Association for the restoration of the exiles and Drummond (or MacGregor) of Balhaldie was sent across to France to the Chevalier[108]to acquaint him with their projects.

Islay, on one occasion, accused Simon of making his house a hotbed of rebellion. 'Calumnies and lies,' answered Lovat hotly, 'Walpole had greater reason to be a Jacobite than I.' The administration was, however, becoming increasingly suspicious of his loyalty, however cleverly he may have masked his disaffection. In 1739 he lost his sheriffship and his pension and his company was taken from him. It was then that the Black Watch Regiment was formed and immediately dispatched, perhaps to keep it out of mischief at home.

Next year Lovat received his patent from France for the Dukedom, which he apparently coveted so much: Duke of Fraser, Marquis of Beaufort, Earl of Stratherrick and Abertarff, Viscount of the Aird and Strathglass, Earl Lovat of Beauly[109] – a sufficiently grandiose title surely to satisfy the most ambitious of vain human beings. In 1743 he was appointed, by James, Lord Lieutenant North of the Spey.

When, however, Prince Charlie landed, Lovat was greatly annoyed by the suddenness of his arrival and the manner of it. He did not land like a prince, he said; he had no forces, only a few servants. Writing to Lochiel, who felt it incumbent upon him to stand by his Prince in his daring enterprise, Lovat says: 'I fear you have been ower-rash in going ere affairs are ripe; I'll aid when I can but my prayers are all I can give at present. My service to the Prince but I wish he had not come here so empty-handed. Silver would go far in the Highlands.'

To others Lovat spoke of the Prince as a 'mad, unaccountable gentle-

---

108 Chevalier de St Georges or the Old Pretender; the names given to James Stuart, son of James II of Great Britain and Ireland, deposed in 1688.
109 Ruvigny's *Jacobite Peerage*, p. 56.

man' and, in answer to a letter from the Lord Advocate, reminding him of former services rendered and hoping he would show his old zeal on behalf of the Government, he writes: 'Your Lordship judges right when you believe that no hardship or ill-usage that I meet with can alter or diminish my zeal and attachment to His Majesty's person and Government.' He complains, however, that his clan are unarmed and asks for a thousand stand of arms immediately that he may see how he will exert himself in the King's service. Needless to say, the arms were not sent.

From September, 1743 onward we find him in almost daily correspondence with Culloden or with Lord Loudoun, the Commander of the Inverness Garrison. The two urge him to exert himself against the rebels, and the old man excuses himself with painstaking, long-winded ingenuity on the plea of his own ill-health and for other specious reasons. After the victory of Prestonpans, he became somewhat bolder. He sent the fiery cross round, equipped 700 Frasers and compelled his elder son to go at their head to join the Prince.

Of course, these proceedings could not be hidden from Loudoun and Culloden, but Simon still believed in his ability to hoodwink them. He speaks to them of the insolent behaviour of his son to himself and his mad behaviour to the Government; of his inability to persuade him, 'for he laughs at me when I make strong remonstrance against his resolutions.' He speaks of his son's influence with the Clan being ten times greater than his own and of his resolution, since he has no strength to mount on horse-back, to live peaceably in his house as a faithful subject to the King and to keep his own country free from robbers, thieves and loose men. About the same time he is writing to Prince Charlie that it is the greatest grief of his life that he is unable to join his dear, brave Prince but he is sending his eldest son, the hope of his family and the darling of his life, to venture his last drop of blood in the glorious Prince's service. With him he is sending two handsome battalions, well armed and equipped; only a few old gentlemen, infirm like himself, being left at home.

At length, on 11th December, 1745, Loudoun marched with 800 men to Castle Dounie and brought Lovat to Inverness as a sort of hostage for the fidelity of the portion of his clan that had not marched with his son. But Loudoun soon discovered that he had laid hold of a slippery prisoner. By an artful device, Lovat succeeded in delaying his commitment to Inverness Castle and one night made his escape from the house in which he was temporarily confined. In January we find him receiving congratulations from Lochiel, Cluny MacPherson (his son-in-law) and Murray of Broughton,[110] who were with Prince Charlie. They urge on him the expediency of appearing openly for the Prince and even offer him the command of the Army, for they feel certain that his advice and counsel 'will be of greater value than several thousand men.' Lovat, however, apart from physical disability, was not prepared to take such a decided step. He preferred to give his sympathy and best wishes and to watch events from the safe house of his kinsman, Fraser of Gortuleg, near Foyers.[111]

From his refuge in Stratherrick he writes to his son about preparing a hiding place in the Isle of Muilly[112] in Glen Strathfarrar. But by this time the fortunes of the rebellion were waning; the retirement northward from Derby, with Cumberland following after, told its own tale. Perhaps with the hope of escaping out of the toils and making peace with the Government before it was too late, he sent another message to his son to come north under pretext of raising more men. He could then assure Culloden that he had recalled him to his duty. But the high-spirited youth wrote back: 'That I should at such a critical time run home would look ill; and the pretext, as it would be called, of raising men, would not screen me from the imputation your Lordship, I am sure, would wish me to shun. I am persuaded that your people will come up to a man if you order them.'

Northward, meanwhile, the Jacobite army retreated until the stand was made on Culloden's fatal field. From that field Prince Charlie fled with a few followers toward Stratherrick and so to Gortuleg House, where he spent the night and, for the first and last time, met Lord Lovat. It is said that the latter tried to encourage the Prince to continue the struggle. 'Remember your great ancestor Robert Bruce,' he is reported to have said, 'who lost eleven battles and won Scotland by the twelfth.'

But next day Charles fled westward toward the wilds of Lochaber, and apparently Lovat followed, for Murray of Broughton tells of a

---

110 Not to be confused with the Murrays of Broughton and Cally (Broughton House, Nat Trust for Scotland). Sir John took his name from his partimony of Broughton in Peeblesshire; his house was burnt by accident in 1773 and is now only a ruin (Alan McNie *Clan Murray* 1988).
111 Probably Gorthleck House.
112 Not so named in OS maps, but the River Farrar has a small island-dominated lochan called Loch a' Mhuillidh (see Places Index).

gathering of the rebel chiefs at Muirlagan on Loch Arkaigside – the Lochiel country – when Simon harangued them on the duty of dying sword in hand, rather than yield. But rhetoric of this kind, especially from a man like Lovat, was useless mockery when it was evident that all was lost. The soldiers of Butcher Cumberland were already burning and ravaging the Highland glens – the Aird and Castle Dounie among the rest – and resistance was hopeless.

Simon was carried – he was now unable to walk – from one place to another, probably by Loch Arkaig and Glen Pean down to Loch Morar, on an island in which he found refuge for a month. But information of his movements had somehow leaked out. Sloops with soldiers were sent from Fort William round to search Arisaig and Moidart, and in one of their descents Simon was discovered. One rather dubious tradition says that he was hiding in a hollow tree from which his great legs, swathed in flannel, protruded. The more authentic account, quoted in *The Scots Magazine* of 1747, reports that he was found lying on two feather beds trying to keep himself warm.

Looking North over the Sands of Morar towards the hills of North Morar and Knoydart. This narrow bar of sand, crossed by the Mallaig 'Road to the Isles', separates secluded Loch Morar from the Atlantic Ocean. (Photo by Reginald Fry)

He was conveyed in a litter to Fort William, whence he wrote a pleading letter to Cumberland in which he recalled the fact that he had carried the Duke in his arms, when a child, in Kensington Park and said: 'I can do more service to the King and Government than the destroying of a hundred such old men like me, past seventy without the use of hands, legs and knees.' But he might as well have appealed to Ben Nevis as to that hard, pitiless heart.

From Fort William he was taken by litter to London. Hogarth saw him at the White Hart Inn, St Albans and painted the well-known portrait of him. As he approached the Tower he saw the scaffold erected for the execution of Kilmarnock and Balmerino and reading there his own fate, treated his attendants with a train of reflections on the strange vicissitudes of his life – his hardships among the mountains in his youth, his adventures abroad, his intimacy with distinguished foreigners, his greatness and now his fall. He was an eloquent moraliser and deeply impressed those who heard him.

At his trial, which began on 9th March, 1747, his conduct was that of a dignified old man, persecuted by fate and oppressed by bitter enemies. Sometimes he was pathetic, sometimes indignant but never captious or querulous.[113] The two chief witnesses against were both traitors, his own secretary, Robert Fraser and Prince Charlie's secretary, Murray of Broughton and in his written defence he denounced Murray as 'the most abandoned of mankind who, forgetting his allegiance to his King and country has ... endeavoured to destroy both,' and then 'imprudently appears at your lordships' bar, to betray those very secrets he had drawn from the person he called his lord, his prince and master, under the greatest confidence.'[114]

On 18th March he was unanimously found guilty and next day sentence of death was pronounced. After receiving the sentence he made a short appeal to both Houses of Parliament, to intercede for the mercy of the Crown. When asked if he had anything further to say, he replied: 'Nothing but to thank your lordships for your goodness to me. God bless you all and I bid you an everlasting farewell: we shall not meet all in the same place again – I am sure of that.' When the Major of the Tower

---

113 Fond of raising objections and argumentative.
114 Quotations here appear to be from *State Trials*.

came to visit him in his cell a few days before his execution and asked how he did, he answered: 'Why pretty well, I am preparing myself, sir, for a place where hardly any majors and very few lieutenant-generals go.' And to the young barber who came to shave him on the morning of his journey to the scaffold, he expressed the hope 'to be in heaven by one o'clock, or I should not be so merry now.'

He expressed a wish that his body should be buried in Kirkhill and said that he had left in his will a sum to pay all the pipers from John O'Groats House to Edinburgh, to play before his body, and the old women would wail the Coronach and then there would be crying and clapping of hands 'for I am one of the greatest chiefs in the Highlands'.[115] He desired the attendance of a Roman Catholic chaplain and declared that he died in that faith.[116] For thirty years he had been by repute a Presbyterian, though he had no great regard for ministers, but in the end he evidently wanted to make the future secure and so nailed his religious colours to the mast. At midday on 9th April the tragedy was ended.

He went to the scaffold without trepidation. 'Do you think I am afraid of an axe?' he said. 'It's a debt we all must pay and don't you think it better to go off in this manner than to linger with consumption, gout, dropsy or fever?' Tremendous interest was taken in him and his execution and for tens of thousands his death was a spectacle and a holiday. When he reached the scaffold he looked round and said: 'God save us! Why should there be a bustle about taking off an old grey head that can't get up three steps without two men to support it?' He felt the edge of the axe and examined his coffin with its simple inscription. He uttered the Horatian motto: *'Dulce et Decorum est pro patria mori'*, followed by a line of Ovid's, despairing of the futile actions of his ancestors who sought the freedom and independence of his homeland. He then embraced one of his clansmen before laying his head on the block and at one blow it was severed.

Two of his clansmen tried to get his body to be carried by ship to Inverness, thence to Kirkhill, but at the last moment the Government

---

115 *Scots Magazine* 1747 p. 155.

116 This chaplain, a Mr Baker from the Sardinian Embassy, also wrote a full and authentic *Candid Account* of the last six days of Lovat's life in the Tower (see McLaren 1957).

intervened and refused permission. Almost certainly they were afraid of the effect of his funeral on his clansmen. At any rate, he was buried in the Tower on 17th April and his bones were transferred to the Chapel crypt there in 1877, along with the other Jacobite Lords beheaded earlier.[117]

Simon's personal appearance is presented to us, in his old age, in Hogarth's masterly portrait. There we have the massive figure with his broad forehead, knit into large knots as by concentration on the working out of his tortuous schemes; the eyes widely apart, blinking with a light half fierce, half humorous; the flat, somewhat misshapen nose, the broad mouth expanding in a smile of cajolery. Dr Carlyle of Inveresk speaks of him as 'tall and stately (and might have been handsome in his youth) with a very flat nose. His manners were not disagreeable, though his address consisted chiefly in gross flattery and in the due application of money.'[118]

His character is writ large in his actions. He seemed to be a lover of the crooked, and although he went so far as to assert that he never betrayed a private man or a public cause, he was no competent judge of his own actions. There are more ways than one of not letting your right hand know what your left hand is doing and Lovat had chosen the way of deceit. His public speech and action were no criterion of what the other man within was thinking and devising, and this dual personality was responsible for strange results.

He was born in an age when the principles of Macchiavelli, that it is necessary to be a master in feigning and dissembling in order to achieve your ends, were applied to politics, and he had deeply imbibed these principles. He found how easily men could be duped and flattered, so he did not hesitate to make large use of flattery and deceit and, in

---

117 There remains the rumour, still believed by some locally, that the Laird's remains were somehow smuggled, possibly by exchange with another body, to Inverness on board *The Pledger* and buried at Kirkhill. However, McLaren – whose great-great-great-grandfather was master of *The Pledger*, assures us (p. 228) that the rumour was merely an intention stated in the shipmaster's letter to a friend in Inverness and not an accomplished fact. Mackenzie 1936, pp. 180–1 quotes the authority of the Tower Chaplain for the London burial, with the additional information (from Henrietta Taylor in *Scottish Historical Review*, Jan 1928) that the initial granting of the body to the Frasers was rescinded when General Williamson, Governor of the Tower, complained to Lord Cornwallis that they were 'making a show of the body for money'.
118 Quoted from Clerk's *Memoirs*.

doing so, he lost moral sensibility and judged the good of anything by the measure of its success. He was quite prepared to take any road that promised success, and having been thrown, in his youth, into positions of difficulty and danger, he learned the fox's cunning and craft as a means of escape. Balhaldie writes of him, after his execution, as 'one who never lost the point he had in view; whose surprising presence of mind, in all wants, gave occasion to his seizing opportunities for succeeding in things by the ablest thought impracticable.'

Behind this indiscriminate panegyric lies the truth that, by being indifferent as to the means he used and by using language not to reveal but to conceal his thoughts, for a time he succeeded. And being obsessed by his own cleverness, he became almost convinced of his own sincerity and rectitude. He was impatient of fine moral reflections and sentiments because they did not win a case or gain an estate. So with great presence of mind he snatched at the readiest means that promised success.

He must not be condemned, however, as if he were unlike others of his age. 'He lived in times of constant political unrest, when men wore Stuart coats one day and Hanoverian the next; when even ministers sold secrets to the other court; when men, uncertain as to the future and anxious to retain their estates, kept a foot in either camp, stopped at home as loyal citizens themselves, and let their sons lead clansmen to fight on the other side.'

Behind all Lovat's scheming and twisting and shifting in speech and action there must have been certain master-motives or emotions. What were they? I suggest pride and hunger of heart. He was intensely proud of his family, of his ancestral history; inordinately vain of being '*Mac-Shimi na H-Aird*'.[119] He hungered first to get possession of the position

---

119 'Son of Simon of the Aird' – there have been many Simon Lovats over their 750 year history, some more famous than others. But the family trace their origins to one Simon, given the Lordship of Lovat by Alexander II in c.1248. The present heir, another Simon, inherited the title at the age of 18 in 1995, again under tragic circumstances. In 1994 his father died of a heart attack while riding near Beaufort Castle just days after his brother had been gored to death by a buffalo in Tanzania. One year later, the mantle of responsibility fell to Simon on the death, at 83, of his grandfather Lord 'Shimi' Lovat, a hero of the Normandy D-Day landings (see William MacKay 1905, pp. 53–60 and *The Daily Telegraph* 21.8.97 & 8.12.98).

that he felt belonged of right to him; a position of honour and affluence where he could dispense the patriarchal, unlimited hospitality and exercise the unregulated authority of a Highland chief, and then to make himself in rank and territory and power the greatest MacShimi that ever existed. That is the secret of his restless activity, of his political scheming, of his changing sides so often. That was the spark that ignited the heather in the autumn of his life and ended, as it was bound to do, in tragedy.

Chapter 5

The Dove of Iona

St Columba, or Columcille as he was known to his own countrymen, may be called Primus Scotorum in a double sense: the first of Scots in the older meaning of that name, for up till the twelfth century Scot and Scotia meant Irish and Ireland, and in its later meaning as the first of Scotsmen.

There were kings before Agamemnon and Christian saints in Scotland like Ninian,[120] Kentigern,[121] Palladius[122] and others before Columba, but they are names or legendary figures dimly seen through the mists of antiquity. It is otherwise with St Columba. The light of history presents him to our view, a living august personality, commanding our admiration and reverence. He, more than any other, shaped the course of our Scottish history and gave the impetus that lifted the people from gross barbarism to civilisation.

Our original authorities for the career of this man consist of two 'Lives' written by successors of his in the Abbey of Iona: Cummian,[123] the seventh and Adamnan,[124] the ninth Abbot. The former account was written about sixty years after St Columba's death, the latter about one hundred, but both must have known some who had seen and conversed with the Saint and, in a small community like that of Iona and among a people so tenacious of traditions as they were, remembrances of him would be vividly retained. While wonders connected with him would naturally tend to grow, yet beneath these would subsist a body of historic facts.

---

120 St Ninian set up a monastery at Whithorn in Galloway in 396, from which he evangelised much of Southern Pictland and probably had influence in Ireland.

121 Also known as St Mungo, Kentigern (b 514) came from a Christian group under St Serf at Fife to establish the cathedral church at Glasgow.

122 Palladius' influence was mainly in Ireland, to which he was sent as its first official bishop by Pope Celestine in 430.

123 Known as Cummian the Fair, Abbot 657–669, wrote *On the Virtues of St Columba*.

124 Abbot 679–704, wrote *Life of St Columba*, probably during this period.

8th century Font of Adamnan, Columba's successor, outside the entrance of Fortingall Church. Adamnan reputedly spent his final years in Glen Lyon, being buried at Craig Pheannaidh near Glen Lyon Church.

Adamnan has incorporated in his own 'Life' most of that recorded by his predecessor, Cummian. A manuscript of this 'Life' belonging to the old Irish monastery of Reichman is preserved in the public library of Schaffhausen and belongs, apparently, to the beginning of the eighth century, almost to the very date at which it was written. The Colophon[125] mentions that it was written by one, Dorbherne, and we know that one of that name was *fear-leughaidh* (Reader) and, afterwards, Abbot of Iona in 713, nine years after the death of Adamnan. It is very probable that it was he who wrote this copy and that it was carried away from Iona when the monks fled, taking every precious thing they could carry with them, from the incursions of the Norsemen, who burnt the Abbey in 795.

In the seventh and eight centuries, the active, restless, ardent spirit of these Celtic monks of Ireland and Scotland carried them away from

---

125 Like a title page, giving scribe or printer's name, date, etc, but appearing at the end of the book.

their own homes to seek, in distant lands and islands, opportunities of devotion and of carrying to others the Gospel, which had lighted such a flame of heavenly fire within their own land and hearts. In Germany[126] and Switzerland religious communities were established by them, which became centres of enlightenment and piety to the rough peoples around them. Thus the oldest Irish writings come to us now, not from Ireland, but from Switzerland and Italy, where these Irish monks, writing their Latin mass, put in the margin Irish translations of words and phrases.

When the monks of Iona could no longer remain safely in their own dearly loved little Isle, some of them fled to Dunkeld; others sought refuge and opportunity of labour with their brethren in the wilds of the Swiss mountains. Here, far from the place where its subject and its author had lived and laboured, this precious 'Life' found a safe resting place and has been preserved.

Though called a Life of St Columba, it is not in strict form a biography at all, such as we have in Boswell's *Johnson* or Southey's *Life of Wesley*. Its purpose is to glorify the Saint and demonstrate his possession of such supernatural powers as were considered necessary to prove his title to saintship, rather than to give us a record of his life. It is a collection in three books of the prophecies, the miracles and the visions of the Saint. While such a form precluded any orderly or detailed account of his life, and immediately raises our suspicions in regard to the authenticity of the events recorded, it yet affords us an extensive knowledge of his activities, his habits of life and his character, as well as a living picture of the community over which he presided.

As through the *Little Flowers of St Francis*[127] we get a true knowledge of the personality of that meekest and gentlest of saints, so from the prophecies and miracles of this 'Life' St Columba is clearly presented to us. In addition to St Adamnan's 'Life', there are other more or less reliable sources of information in old Irish 'Lives', which help to fill up the general details of his career, thus enabling us to possess a more

---

126 E.g. the convent at Erfurt, from which came Martin Luther, is believed to have been a Celtic foundation (McNeill 1920 p. 35).

127 Legends about the life of St Francis of Assisi, collected into an early biography (or hagiography) and translated from Latin into Italian in the 14th century.

authentic portrait of the man, his character and labours, than of any individual of that age belonging to these islands.

St Columba was born about the year AD 521, at Gartan[128] in Donegal. On both his father's and his mother's side he was of royal lineage, his father being the great-grandson of one of the most famous ancient Irish kings, Niall of the Nine Hostages. He belonged to the powerful clan of the O'Donnels, who held sway in that part of Ireland. Scarcely one hundred years before, St Patrick[129] had landed in Ireland, advanced to Tara,[130] its Capital, and given a bold challenge to Druidism. His very daring impressed the King and princes, so that they readily listened to his message and, with Celtic impetuosity, accepted it without, indeed, realising what its requirements were.

Like one of our Highland moor fires in the spring, the new faith swept over the land till the wildest parts of the west accepted it with a fervour or enthusiasm peculiar to an emotional people. Another reason for this easy victory of Christianity was the existence of the clan system and the submission of the clansmen to their chiefs. St Patrick and his fellows did not direct their preaching to convince the people but the chiefs, knowing that if they should succeed in gaining them, the rest was easy; the people would necessarily follow. Even in later times, this submission to the chief in matters of religion is apparent. The islands are Protestant or Catholic today just as the chiefs happened to be in the seventeenth century. So, in the wilds of Donegal, where this child was born, Christianity, at least in form, held sway and he was baptised by the name of Colum, a dove.

It was the custom in Ireland in those days – a custom which continued in our own Highlands down to the eighteenth century – for the sons of chiefs to be sent out to foster-parents to be nurtured and trained. (The devotion of foster-brothers to their chief in battle is famous in

---

128 At Church Hill, near Lough Gartan.

129 It is interesting to note that Patrick (or Phadraig) was a Briton, probably born in Dumbarton, who may have received some Christian instruction in Gaul before being captured in Wales by Irish invaders. He is certainly more acceptable, therefore, as a Celtic missionary to the Celts than is Palladius, the Pope's apostle to the Celts, who arrived about the same time.

130 The Hill of Tara, near Trim, 21 mls NW of Dublin is reputedly the site of the original 'Coronation Stone' on which the High Kings of Ireland were crowned.

Highland story.) Columba was entrusted to the care of one, Cruith-nechan (The Little Pict), who was a local priest, and by him he was taught and trained in the Christian Faith and pious acts in that age of youthful enthusiasm for Christianity.

The boy proved an apt pupil. Like Samuel from his boyhood, he lived in the sanctuary, loved its services, particularly its music, and was assiduous in study. Of a poetical temperament – afterwards himself a hymn writer – he took particular delight in the Psalter. It appealed to his aesthetic sense, as well as to the fervour of his devotion. Its poetry was so high and pure beside the rough bardism of his day. One explanation of his name, Colum-cille – Colum of the Church – is that he was so called by the other boys when they saw how he frequented the church to learn and sing the Psalms.

When he grew up to early manhood and had now definitely dedicated himself to the services of the Church, he was sent to one of the great monastic schools for which Ireland was then famous, that of Moville under St Finnian. From there, he went to a still more famous school, that of Clonard, which had been founded by another St Finnian. At this monastic institution, as many as three thousand are said to have gathered at one time and, after making allowance for exaggeration, the numbers who came together to these schools is remarkable. It shows how thousands, wearied of the rough, ignorant, fighting life of these fierce times, were drawn to the new learning and culture promoted under the Christian Faith, and to the higher and more fruitful form of life it fostered. A new outlook and enthusiasm was given to the youth of Ireland and they responded to that.

Outside these communities, the old fighting went on almost unabated; the tribal wars were as fierce and brutal as ever. Within the community, behind the cashel or rampart of the monastery, was a place of calm in the midst of the storm, a place of aspiration and knowledge, of enlargement of mind, of heavenly hopes, of brotherhood and industry, not of strife and destruction.

Different ages of religion have different modes for giving expression to it and, during the fourth and fifth centuries, the favourite mode was the monastic. Thus the Celtic Church, as we see it at Clonard and elsewhere in Ireland and afterwards at Iona, being a product of the fifth century, had this monastic character strongly, even peculiarly impressed on it.

Monasticism had its rise in Egypt and was due, in large part, to the religious mood of the East, which found in solitary contemplation and ascetic mysticism the highest type of piety. The first monks were solitary recluses, who fled out to the desert to escape the evil of the world and perfect themselves in devotion and holy contemplation. Gradually, these recluses drew together and formed themselves into communities under the rule of a father (Abba). This monasticism spread westward through Marseille into France – John Cassian (AD 415) and Martin of Tours (AD 372)[131] – and thence to Wales – St David – and Ireland. In this movement it acquired a somewhat different character, becoming less contemplative and more practical. The monasteries were like oases in the desert, centres not only of unworldly devotion but also of peaceful industry, where a new lifestyle was propagated. Learning and agriculture went hand in hand so that, in modern Gaelic, the word once used for scholar or disciple has come to mean a ploughman; zeal for the Faith was joined to protection for the weak.

As we have said, however, even after Ireland was nominally converted to Christianity, little change took place in the general character of the people. The clans still raided and fought each other; a man was still held in esteem as he could drink quaichs of strong drink and crush heads; law and order was held in low esteem. Under these conditions it was almost hopeless to propagate Christianity, except by forming communities of Christians who could dwell together in comparative security, protected by the fear belonging to sanctity; who could be subject to Christian law and present a model of what Christian civilisation meant. The same thing is seen in the approach to mission in Africa at Lovedale, Blantyre and elsewhere. In fact, the great Scottish missionaries, like Drs Stewart, Scott and Law,[132] simply revived the old system we see in Ireland in Columba's day. There the choice, high-souled youth

---

131 St Ninian was a great disciple of St Martin and dedicated his stone church, which stonemasons from Tours had helped to construct at Whithorn, to his memory in 400, the year of the patriarch's death.

132 Missionaries involved in setting up schools in East Africa, such as the Lovedale Institute in the 19th century. James Stewart (see note 36) was Principal there from 1857 and a few years before his death gave a lecture in Edinburgh entitled 'Dawn in the Dark Continent' (pub. 1903). The Author may well have attended this lecture as a young minister and graduate of the University.

of the land, like Columba himself, were trained in a new life in communities which became, as Dr Johnson says, 'luminaries radiating forth the benefits of knowledge and the blessings of religion.'

Many of those belonging to these religious communities were content to continue without clerical rank or title, but Columba, in virtue of his noble birth as well as of his ardour, was evidently marked out for authority and honour. It is said that, while he was studying at Clonard, St Finnian, perceiving his remarkable talents, was anxious that he should be consecrated bishop and attached to his own community for episcopal functions. For this purpose he sent him to one Etchen, a bishop whom Columba found ploughing and by whom he was, by mistake it is said, simply ordained priest. The fact of his ordination by this man is probably true; the rest of the story was probably composed to explain why so famous a man was never given bishop's orders.

While yet a young man, he was acquiring a reputation for learning, for zeal, for fearless denunciation of wrong. In such a rude age as that, commanding fearlessness, which was not afraid to face up to any man and dared to rebuke the powerful, was bound to win for a man reputation and honour. He that could smite the wrongdoer and shield the weak would be revered as a saint.

Columba was also believed to possess extraordinary powers. We read how on one occasion, while studying with Gemman, an old bard, a little girl came flying toward them pursued by her master, who in his fury killed her as she clung to the old man. 'How long,' cried Gemman, 'will God leave this horrible deed unrevenged?' 'This same hour,' said Columba, 'in which the soul of this murdered girl ascends to heaven, will the soul of that murderer descend to hell.' And at the word, like Ananias before Peter, that murderer of the innocent fell down dead in their presence. The report of this sudden and terrible judgment spread through all the provinces of Ireland, says Adamnan, carrying with it the fame of the young deacon. And when once he was believed to possess these praeternatural powers, even ordinary prescience and reasonable consequences would be magnified into marvellous gifts of prophecy and miracle in an age which looked to its holy men having these extraordinary gifts of the Spirit.

Nor are we to dismiss such things as are recorded of men evidently moved by the highest spiritual influences, as was St Columba, by a cheap sneer at credulity and superstition. The fact also of his royal lineage helped to give him honour and pre-eminence among a people accustomed to reverence princely ancestry. The clan spirit dominated everything; the spirit of rule and leadership was in his blood; so at an early age, not yet twenty-five, he began to assume the office of leader and to found religious communities under himself.

The first of these was at Derry and, some years afterwards, he founded another at Durrow. Although St Columba's name is pre-eminently – almost exclusively nowadays – connected with Iona, yet his heart was knit to these two places in his own beloved Ireland as it never was to Iona. Often, in Iona, we find his thoughts back in Derry and some verses still extant express the strength of his love for it, because of its quietness and purity, as if full of white angels. It would be only natural that one of such an energetic and adventurous spirit should look out beyond the bounds of his own land and that the claims of the heathen would appeal to him, as they did to others of his countrymen. And almost at the door there was a great field for Christian enterprise.

Irish emigrants had gone forth from the north of Ireland sixty years before, under the leadership of Fergus MacErc, had invaded the western seaboard of Scotland and conquered that part of it called *Earra-Ghaidheal* (Argyle), the land of the Gridel. That territory was then called Dalriada, after their old home in Ireland.[133] As our own colonists and ex-patriots require some to minister to them in holy things in their new homes, so did these Dalriadans. Beyond them, threatening their very existence, was the larger field of Northern Pictland, scarcely penetrated, if at all, by Christian missionaries. One like Columba could scarcely rest satisfied with building on other men's foundations. Like St Paul, that first great Christian missionary, he must have wistfully looked out to new lands – and here in Scotland was his opportunity. His own countrymen needed one to keep them from lapsing back altogether into heathenism, and the Picts required a missionary to evangelise them.

Another fact that may have drawn attention to Scotland, about the year 560, was that the Dalriadans had just suffered a severe defeat at

---

133 The Dal Riata were Gaels originally from Antrim. Other Irish settlements, dating from about 500, are found in SW Scotland, North Wales and SW England (Foster *Picts, Gaels & Scots* 1996, Historic Scotland series).

The ruined church of Lawers, built in 1669 at the water's edge on Loch Tay. According to local Gaelic legend, its destruction by a storm in 1833 – 'when [the tree] reaches the gable the church will be split asunder' – was one of the many prophecies made in the late 17th century by the Lady of Lawers.

the hands of the Pictish King, Brude. There is, in my opinion, no reason to doubt that the supreme motive causing Columba to exile himself – for so it seemed to him – was love for the souls of men. But so intense was his love for his own land and people that contributory causes were needed to bring him to a decision, and I think there must, therefore, be some measure of truth in the ancient Irish account of the immediate cause of his sailing for Scotland. It certainly sounds a sufficiently Irish cause, if our Celtic brethren will excuse the joke, for initiating a great missionary undertaking.

In the year 561, a sanguinary battle was fought, at a place called Culdremhue,[134] between the Clan Neill of Ulster and Diarmid, King of Ireland. The quarrel which occasioned this battle is said to have originated in a dispute between Columba and St Finnian of Moville.

---

134 The site of the 'Battle of the Book' is now known as Cooldrumman, near Drumcliff, 5 miles north of Sligo.

The former had borrowed a Psalter from St Finnian, in order to copy it, but when he brought the original back to its owner, Finnian claimed the copy also as his. This early dispute of copyright was appealed by both to King Diarmid, who gave his decision against Columba, with the words: 'To every cow its calf and to every book its copy.' The apparent injustice of this decision stirred the old proud, passionate nature of the princely Columba like a slumbering wolf, and also stirred the ire of his fellow clansmen, who had other causes of quarrel against the King.

It is said that, for stirring up strife and causing such loss of life, Columba was arraigned before a synod and for a time excommunicated. There is no doubt he was, at some time, excommunicated for a short period, for Adamnan mentions this, though without giving the cause. He also pointedly mentions this battle as preceding Columba's mission to Scotland. It is further said that, in order to expatiate his outburst of passion and to bring to Christ, from the deathly state of heathenism, as many as had been slain on the field of battle, he resolved to exile himself from Ireland.

Whatever the immediate cause, in the spring of the year 563, two years after the Battle of Culdremhue, as Adamnan mentions three times, Columba with twelve companions set sail in their skin coracles for Scotland. Legend reports that he first landed in Colonsay and finding that from it the shore of Ireland was still visible, he sailed further until he next reached the little island of Iona. Landing at the bay still called *Port na curraich*, he ascended the hillock overlooking it – *Càrn cul ri Eirinn* (the Cairn of the back to Erin) – and, seeing no trace of Ireland on the horizon, he resolved to settle in this isle.

Iona, as you know, is a small island lying off the south-west point of Mull, about four miles in length by one in breadth. It is a rocky, treeless island, exposed to the full fury of the south-west gales. Two thirds of the Island consists of bare rock and peat moss but at the north-west end, where the monastery was situated, there is some fertile land and, opposite this on the western side of the Island, there is a fairly broad stretch of sandy plain, or *machair*. Here then, St Columba and his companions made their new home.

We can picture to ourselves its character. Firstly, they built themselves some beehive shaped huts of wattle and turf; then they laboriously cut down wood in the neighbouring Island of Mull, conveyed it across the sound and proceeded to build a church. Afterwards other buildings, such as guest houses, barns, kilns, etc. were built, and round about those buildings a rampart of earth was raised, although it would avail little protection to them.

To us it seems strange that a little, out-of-the-way island like that should be chosen as a new centre from which Christian truth and civilisation was to radiate. Probably they were chiefly swayed in their choice by the two thoughts of seclusion and safety; the desire to mark their separation from the world and to have a quiet home to which they could return from the hardships and dangers of further excursions.

After spending two years in organising matters in Iona, Columba resolved to attack the very centre of Pictish heathenism by going to the capital of King Brude at Inverness. If the King were converted to the Christian Faith the people, accustomed to submitting to the authority of princes and chiefs, would speedily follow. So taking two companions, Columba set out on the long and perilous journey, taking their own coracle with them to carry them over the lochs of the Great Glen. Where King Brude's castle exactly was, it is now impossible for us to say – Dr Reeves supposed CraigPhatrick, Dr Skene suggests Torvean.

Apparently the Druids with the King got intelligence of Columba's approach and conceiving him to be the powerful magician of a new god, they represented him to Brude as one who had come from an enemy's land and race to injure him by his malign spells. So when Columba approached the castle, they found the gates shut against them. But the saint, says Adamnan, went boldly forward and laid his hand upon the gate which at his touch immediately flew open. The King on learning what had happened, was filled with fear. So out he went with his counsellors to meet the holy man and received him with all respect and ever afterwards, held him in great veneration.

The Druids having so far failed, tried other measures to defeat his purpose. When the Saint and his companions were engaged at evening worship, according to their practice, some of the Druids drew near and began to make a noise, to disturb and silence them. At this Columba, who was possessed of a magnificent voice – clear, musical and powerful – began to sing the 45th Psalm: '*Eructavit cor meum verbum bonum: dico ego opera mea regi.*' ('My heart is inditing a good thing: I speak of my works for the king.')[135] And so wonderful did his voice sound, like thunder above them, that they were terrified and fled.

I have heard it said that, when the great Dr MacDonald of Ferintosh was preaching in the open air on the south side of the Cromarty Firth, many gathered on the opposite side to listen to him. St Columba's voice could carry a long distance, so that when the monks were harvesting on the *machair*, on the west side of Iona, sometimes on a still autumn day they heard him singing the Psalms within the church, nearly a mile away.

Although we are not expressly told that King Brude accepted the Christian Faith, yet the veneration in which he held St Columba, the intercourse which subsisted between them for years and the freedom with which the Saint was permitted to travel and preach throughout the Pictish Kingdom, all tend to show that he came to accept it. But the respect shown by the King naturally exasperated the Druids and particularly Broichan, the chief Druid and the King's foster-father. When Columba turned homeward, Broichan boasted that he would bring down a storm of wind and thick mist upon Loch Ness, which would prevent his sailing. The wind and thick rain did, indeed, come down from the west on the day, but then Broichan was not so experienced in sailing as the man he intended to baffle. When, therefore, the Saint fearlessly launched his little boat and sped away, apparently in the teeth of the wind, poor Broichan was left speechless on the strand.

After this we find Columba, on more than one occasion, visiting Inverness. On one of these occasions he had another encounter with Broichan. The Saint asked him to liberate a slave girl he had and, when the request was refused, he declared that before he left the district Broichan would die. That same day, as Columba made his way homeward, two messengers came from the King to report that his foster-father had been taken suddenly ill and was at the point of death. Columba, the record declares, gave them a white stone, which he had blessed, and told them to put it in water and let Broichan drink of it and he would recover, and this is exactly what happened. When, some years later, Brude himself was seized with a severe illness, his courtiers sought

---

135 New Internat Vers: 'My heart is served by a noble theme as I recite my verses for the king.' Psalm 45 v 1.

for this same pebble but it could not be found and consequently the King died.

On one of these journeys they were passing by Glenurquhart when Columba bade his companion hasten, for he saw that an old man of great natural goodness was near to death and he wished to baptise him before he died. So they came to the man's house, Columba told him about God and Christ and, like the Ethiopian Eunuch, the man believed and was baptised, shortly before he passed away. If, as many psychologists are now inclined to think, there be such a possession as second sight, St Columba possessed it. Many incidents are recorded of a certain rapture seizing him and he would report to those about him afterwards that he saw certain things happening in Ireland, or in a distant part of Scotland.[136]

In the course of the thirty years of his life in Scotland, many were his journeys through the country, along the western seaboard as far as Skye, founding churches in Tiree and Islay, eastward across Drumalban[137] into Perthshire, and even to Aberdeenshire according to the Book of Deer.[138] This book tells how Columba and his nephew, Drostan, came from Iona to Aberdeen and founded the monastery at Deer. Adamnan gives us picturesque, life-like glimpses of him in his work at Iona among the brethren, and in his journeyings through the islands and rough-bounds of the West, bringing down blessings upon the merciful and hospitable, so that their corn and cattle were multiplied. At the same time he denounced, with scathing severity, the cruelty of robbers and murderers who ravaged the coasts, so that the judgment of God descended with sudden destruction upon them.

Once in Ardnamurchan, for example, he came upon one of these sea robbers, about to embark with his plunder after wasting that poor

---

136 An interesting study in telepathy and clairvoyance from a Biblical Christian standpoint was given by the late Revd J. Stafford Wright in *What is Man?* (Paternoster 1955) Chs. 5 and 6.

137 *Druim Alban* – 'the mountains of the spine of Britain' – refers to the north-south line of the Highlands that formed an eastern barrier to the Kingdom of Dalraida (cf. modern Breadalbane).

138 This document, now in the Cambridge University Library, is a 9th century Gospel written in Latin, but with Gaelic notes on local land settlements written into the margins in the 12th century.

country. He pleaded with him to restore his spoil; followed him even into the sea beseeching him to do so. When, however, the robber laughed him to scorn, Columba withdrew and, ascending a lofty hill that over-looked the sea, watched the spoiler setting sail for the south. 'See that miserable mamukin,' cried the Saint. 'Today, although it is now so calm, a storm will spring from the north and overwhelm him and his comrades in guilt.' And as he spoke the calm, bright sky began to grow overcast and one of those fierce northerly blasts, which come so suddenly and tempestuously in these seas, swept down upon the boats between Mull and Colonsay and sank them.

So gentle and considerate to all in weakness or poverty, always quick to stretch out a helping hand to the distressed, particularly women and children, he was equally stern in denouncing wrong done by the strong. 'Shall I go to Paradise?' said Aedh (Hugh), King of Ireland to him on one occasion. 'Scarcely,' said Columba, 'unless you repent and show the fruit of good works from this time forward.'

In a vision of a later age, St Columba is represented as tall and stern of countenance and there was need for one who, in an age of brutal barbarities, would stand between the feeble and the ruthless strong and make men fear him, because they believed that he could bring down Divine judgment upon the evil-doer. But, while thus severe upon inhumanity, how kind and hospitable he was in welcoming any Christian worker to Iona; how ready to succour the storm-tossed wanderer; how anxious in his care and instant in his prayer for distant labourers, lying awake at night praying for them when he knew they were out in their frail boats on stormy seas! How eagerly he watched for their coming and how constant was his remembrance of those left behind in Ireland!

And as 'he prayeth best who loveth best all creatures great and small', so do we read, not only of sympathy of the tenderest kind for his brethren, but also of pity for the sea birds that were swept by the storm on to the shores of Iona. One inclement day, as he was walking with one of the brethren and looking out to sea, he saw a crane battling against the tempest and at last falling exhausted on the shore. 'Go to yonder bird,' he said to his companion, 'take it home and nurse it for three days, till it is refreshed and can fly back to the sweet region of Ireland, whence it came.' The brother having duly done as he was requested, Columba blessed him, saying: 'The Lord bless you, my son, because you showed hospitality to a stranger.'

Expressions like these show us how, like St Paul yearning for his own people, Columba loved his native Ireland and all belonging to it best of all. More than once did he visit it, being received with increasing honour by his brethren there. Once, when he visited the monastic establishment of Clonmacnoise,[139] the monks came out to meet him and led him, with hymns and praises, into the church, four of them bearing a canopy under which he walked.

His most memorable visit was in connection with a certain synod held at Drumceatt in 575, when he appeared there with Aidan, King of Dalriada, whom he had consecrated in the previous year as King of Scots at Iona – the first of British Kings to be so consecrated.[140] This Convention had been called by King Aedh, who summoned all the provincial kings, the great chiefs and principal clergy, to consider several important matters. One of the questions raised concerned the Bards, who had become so numerous and so exacting in their demands, and whose tongues were so scathing that some were for abolishing their rights altogether. Columba, who was himself an excellent poet – some of his hymns and poetry in Latin and Gaelic still exist – stood up in their defence, called for reform, not abolition, and was the chief means of saving their rights. The chief poet of Ireland, Dallom Forgaill, thereupon wrote a poem in praise of Columba where he lauds, with poetic ardour and exaggeration, his virtues and services to religion and to Ireland.

But a more important question than this was decided there. The Dalriadan Kingdom of Argyle, being an offshoot of Ireland, was regarded as tributary and, therefore, the Kings of Ireland could claim tribute from

---

139 The most celebrated of monastic sites in Ireland, it was established in 545 by St Ciaran on the east bank of the Shannon, 13 mls. south of Athlone. It quickly became a centre of learning and religious craftsmanship, but has been consistently plundered of its treasures over the centuries and was finally given State protection in 1955.

140 Gerber 1992, quoting Skene on the Council of Dumceat (his spelling) notes that no mention was made by Adamnan of the use of the Stone of Destiny at Aidan's coronation; a surprising omission in view of the Stone's significance to later Scottish and English coronations.

it, although it is unlikely that it was ever paid. Now, Aidan and Columba appeared to claim independence for this kingdom and, after discussion, the claim was granted. This was a historic decision for the future as the descendants of Aidan became, not only Kings of Scotland, but afterwards of England also.

So the years passed for this great man, in journeyings often, in labours abundant, in perils by land and sea but also bringing increasing honour to himself and increasing belief in the Faith he proclaimed. 'It is easy,' to use the eloquent words of Montaleinhert, 'to represent to ourselves the tall old man with his fine and regular features, his sweet and powerful voice, the Irish tonsure high on his shaven head and his long locks falling behind, seated at the stern of his coracle, steering through the misty archipelago and narrow lakes of the north of Scotland and bearing from isle to isle and from shore to shore light, justice and truth, the life of the conscience and the soul.'

Columba appeared to have possessed a splendid constitution. Inured to hardship from his youth, his iron frame seemed to defy inclemency of weather and the ravages of age. In spite of the fatigue and discomforts he had to endure by land and sea, for long his natural force remained almost unabated. But at length age and toil began to tell, the visits to distant parts had to cease, the steps became so feeble that, when in the summer days he wished to see the brethren working out on the *machair*, he had to avail himself of the wagon they used for carrying their corn to the monastery.

Premonitions also of the approaching departure came to him. It was now thirty-four years since he had landed in Iona; years of labour and care, years that resembled the sea that washed that little isle, sometimes calm and iridescent, shimmering and sparkling with unshadowed gladness but very often surly and tempestuous. On a certain day in the month of May 597, he was carried across the island to visit the monks at their spring work. As they gathered with veneration and affection round the old man, he told them that he was now anxious to depart to the Lord and had, indeed, wished that the time of his departure should be in the previous month, about Easter. But in order that their joy should not, at that time, be turned to sadness, he had prayed that he might yet be spared on earth for a few days more.

On the first Saturday of June he went out, leaning on the arm of his

Above: The Abbey Church of Iona, dedicated to the Virgin Mary, mainly built around 1507 on the original site of Columba's monastery.

Right: The statue *Descent of the Spirit*, one of three executed in bronze by Jacques Lipchitz – a practising Jew – and presented to the Iona community in 1958 by Sir John and Lady MacTaggart to express the 'unity of the Spirit' which is the essence of the religious community there. It stands in the centre of the Abbey cloisters. (Photos taken in 1959)

faithful attendant, Diarmid, and reached as far as the granary, where
their corn was stored. Here he expressed fervent gratitude to God that
there was a sufficient supply for the community until the harvest. On
their way home the old man sat down on a stone, where afterwards a
cross was erected. While he was sitting there the white horse, which
they had for carrying the milk between the pasture and the monastery,
came up to him and laid its head upon the Saint's breast and began to
utter plaintive cries, as if grieving for his approaching departure. The
Saint gave it his blessing and rising, he ascended a small eminence
overlooking the monastery. Lifting up his hands, he blessed it, saying:
'Little and poor as this place seems today, yet hereafter, not only Scottish
kings and people but also rulers of other nations, with their subject
peoples, will hold it in high honour and saints of other churches will
greatly venerate it.'

After those words, he went down to his own little hut or cell and
proceeded with the copy of the Psalter he was writing. It was the 34th
Psalm and, when he came to the tenth verse – *They that seek the Lord
shall not lack any good'* – 'Here,' he said, 'I must stop; let Baithene [the
brother appointed to succeed him as Abbot] write what follows.' After
this he went into the church to evening prayers and, on returning to
his cell, lay down to rest. To his attendant he gave a last message for
the brethren, enjoining upon them mutual love and peace. At midnight
when the bell was rung for prayers, he arose quickly, hastened into the
church before the others and fell down on his knees before the altar.
Diarmid, coming more slowly and not seeing him, cried: 'Where are
you, my Father?' No voice answered and, before others entered with
lights, Diarmid, groping in the dark, found him lying on his face. Lifting
him up, he placed his head on his knees. Meanwhile, the others had
entered and St Columba opened his eyes for a moment with a look of
joy, attempted to lift his arms to bless them and then sank back dead.
So passed, without pain or struggle, this great man to his rest.

Concerning his appearance, character and manner of life, we need
add little more beyond transcribing the glowing eulogy of Adamnan.
'He was,' he says, 'angelic in appearance, graceful in speech, holy in
work, excellent in skill, wise in counsel. He would not permit even the
space of an hour to pass without employing it in speaking or reading
or writing or some other form of activity. Amid all his labours and

austerities he still showed a cheerful face, being warm-hearted to all and having his soul filled with the joy of the Holy Spirit.'

In his last hours we see him transcribing the Psalter that he dearly loved from his childhood and he took delight in transcribing it. In the Monastery of Durrow was long preserved a copy which was supposed to have been written by him. It is now in Dublin.[141] The example of the master was followed by the disciples, and in after-times some of the most wonderful work in writing and illuminating manuscripts of the Psalter comes to us from the Columban monasteries.

Regarding the wonders mentioned in his life – of prophecy and miracle – an explanation may be found of many of them in exaggeration and in natural foresight. He foretells that one man will have a favourable wind for the mainland of Lorn today, while another tomorrow will be wafted by it to Tiree; or that a calm will be speedily succeeded by a violent storm. But any experienced sailor on that coast will foretell changes like that with much accuracy. One year, when the monks were unable to sow their corn till June, he foretold a bountiful harvest in August; a result that might well have happened, perhaps did happen that year in the light sandy soil of Iona. Such natural causes will, however, only explain some of the marvels recorded and, after due allowance has been made for the credulous, wonder-loving spirit of the age, a residue remains for which the only justifiable explanation is that this man was endowed with gifts of foresight and power, which are sometimes conferred on a few choice sons of men of great emprise and high devotion.

It is impossible for me to set down or summarise here what Scotland owes to St Columba. He is one of her great epochal men, who have given direction and impulse to the current of her history; who have opened up new realms of truth and honour to be entered into and possessed. Of these epochal men St Columba has attained, as in the record of King David's warriors, to a place among the first three. Not only is his memory blessed, his work still remains. It was from that centre of Christian life and light at Iona, which we owe to Columba, that Scotland was evangelised. The simple, earnest, devoted missionaries

---

141 This manuscript, together with the more famous Book of Kells, are now in the Library of Trinity College, Dublin.

from that island carried their message through district after district of the mainland of Scotland. They dared the rough seas and planted the Faith in the Orkneys and even in lonely St Kilda.[142] They penetrated into England. Through St Aidan they christianised Northumbria and, in fact, the larger part of England was brought to accept the Christian faith through the self-sacrificing labours of those who issued from that Celtic Church, which looked to Iona and St Columba as its fount of origin.[143]

After the battle was fought and won, the Church which looked to Rome for its source and authority took the spoils and dignified itself with the title.[144] But the missionary zeal and methods that won Scotland and most of England had been learnt from the little holy isle of the West and from the ardent spirit of that Celt, whose image still, like Ossian's, seems to haunt the dark lochs and misty glens of Scotland.

---

142 See note 103.

143 In 634 Oswald recovered the kingdom of Northumbria which Edwin had lost to the Briton Cadwalla. Having received part of his education at Iona, Oswald wished to bring his people back to the Christian faith, so immediately invited Aidan from Iona to set up a Christian base there, which he did at Lindisfarne in 635.

144 Sadly, it was the very independence of the Celtic endeavour, coupled with the intransigence of St Augustine (against Pope Gregory's advice) which led to the Council of Whitby in 664. Although this Council dealt seemingly with trivial differences in style between those from Iona and those from Canterbury, it ultimately brought about acceptance of the authority of Rome to the Scottish Church and the decline of Iona's influence (for a full discussion see McNeill 1954 pp. 41–3).

Appendix I

The History of Raining's School[145] (to 1880)

Raining's School is the oldest scholastic institution in Inverness.[146] It is sixty-six years older than the Academy, which was opened in 1792, and the other leading schools are much later than that date. The Central School was erected in 1820, the Merkinch and Dr Bell's in the next two decades and the High School, the Free Church Institution, in 1847.

John Raining, merchant in Norwich, 'a Scotsman, from a Christian and charitable disposition and love of his native country', bequeathed in 1722 the sum of £1,000 to the General Assembly of the Church of Scotland, or their deputies, 'to plant a school in any part of North Britain where they think it most wanted', and to maintain the same for the instruction of 'so many fatherless and other poor children in English, Latine and Arithmetic as the said yearly income will maintain.' If the surplus fund, after paying all legatees, allowed it, Mr Raining bequeathed £200 to be given further to erect the school building, but we are not aware that this money was ever paid.

The General Assembly, in 1724, handed over the bequest and its administration, with the consent of Mr Raining's executors, to the Society in Scotland for Propagating Christian Knowledge, because the Assembly could not so fully look after the affair and Mr Raining's mortification did 'so much coincide with the excellent design of the Society's exertions.' The S.P.C.K. had been in existence then for some twenty years and had been erected into a corporation by letters patent

---

145 This report has already appeared in print in an article entitled 'Raining's School, Inverness: a Seed-bed of Talent' by the Very Revd Thomas M. Murchison, in *Transactions of the Gaelic Society of Inverness*, Vol LII, 1980–82, p. 405. It is there described as a contribution to *The Raining's School Magazine*, Vol I, No 5 and 6 (1887) though, with the author's name unknown, it is ascribed to the Headmaster, Alexander Macbain.

146 This was true at the time of writing, since the Grammar School, founded in 1668, was replaced by the Royal Academy.

in 1709. The field of its operations was more specially the Highlands, where it sent missionaries, erected and maintained schools and, in 1738, got its duties so far extended as to enable it to erect schools for the instruction of children, and especially girls, in some of the necessary and useful arts of life, for they found the Highlands 'in a deplorable condition in respect to industry'. In the middle of the last [eighteenth] century the Society had in the Highlands and Islands some 150 schools attended by about 8,000[147] scholars.

The Society decided to fix the school in Inverness and in October 1726 the Inverness Town Council allocated to them for their school 'four rooms above the Grammar School of Inverness, the whole of the third storey of that building, for a school and master's house,' without rent, to enter at the November following. The Council further offered, if the Society wished to build a school house themselves with Raining's £200, the cheerful vicinity of the 'churchyeard', its 'dick' to be the southern boundary. In 1727 the school was constituted and the Town Council received the Society's regulations in regard to it and promised to look after it.

We hear no more of Raining's School until 1747, when we find that Raining's Charity School 'which has for a long space been kept in this place,' as the Inverness Council Records have it, 'has not yet been established in this place,' nor a school house built for itself according to the mortifier's instructions. A claim was indeed made 'by persons of distinction' that the school be fixed at Fort William. The Inverness Council resented this as being 'very unduly'. At any rate, it retarded the Assembly and the Society in fixing the final resting place of the school. But the Inverness Council brought all their influence and that of the Lord President[148] to bear on their claim and they succeeded.

In 1747 it was decided to build the school house in Inverness and the Council was asked to allocate a piece of ground and grant a charter.

---

147 The typewritten report in the editor's possession has these two numbers written out in words while the article already published has them in figures, an unusual change if the report had been copied by Peter MacGregor from Dr McBain's (or any other author's) account. It is this and similar evidence elsewhere in the report which leads me to suggest Peter MacGregor was, indeed, the 'unknown' author of Thomas Murchison's article.

148 Duncan Forbes of Culloden, then Lord President of the Court of Session.

But things moved slowly in those days and it was not until 1751, after some haggling, that they granted a piece of ground on the Colt or Barn Hill out of the town commonty and bought an additional corner from the Incorporation of Taylors for £25, all of which they gave over to the Assembly and the Society gratis and in perpetuity for a yearly payment, if asked, of 'two shillings Scots money' and 'the scolars appearing before us and our successors in office' in the Town Hall on the first Wednesday of each July at twelve o'clock noon.

In 1752 Mr Adam, the famous eighteenth century architect, made a plan for the school and the Society sent it to the Town Council here to get estimates for it. But it was not until April 1756 that the Society finally contracted with the Town Council to build the school for the estimated sum of £516 1s. 9 $^{11}/_{12}$ d. sterling. The school was finally built in 1756–7 and roads were made to the Hill, one of which was fit for carriages. There was no other house on Barnhill, or the wide expanse of plain around it at that time and for nearly seventy years afterwards, with the possible exception of a thatched cottage or two. But there is now quite a new town sprung up within the last two generations on the Hill and its adjacent plain.

The house that was built in 1757 still remains with little alteration[149] save that it was repaired and re-roofed in 1819 and the staircase porch added about twenty years later. It is the three-storey portion, extending east and west, with its tall gable facing the main body of the town. The larger classroom at its east end, running north and south, was built about 1839–40 and an additional piece was put to the northern end of this larger classroom in 1874, while all the rooms were gutted and repaired and a lobby constructed between the two houses. The infant classroom at the back was built in 1881.

For most of the last [eighteenth] century the educational work of the town was done by three schools. Shaw (1775) says: 'There are in the

---

149 Although correct at the time of the Author's writing, there is now sadly no trace of the building. According to the Gaelic Society's article, the School was transferred, in 1894, to the care of the Inverness School Board which used it for a time as the secondary department of the High School. Although still standing in 1963, and in use as a youth club, by 1978 it had been 'demolished to enlarge a car park'. The site is commemorated now only in the name 'Raining's Stairs', leading from Ardconnel Street to Castle Street.

town a Grammar School and a school for teaching English, Writing, Arithmetic, etc., and the Charity School' of John Raining. The number of school children in the town was close on five hundred.

A peculiarity in the organisation of Raining's School was the dual headmastership. There were until 1846 always two headmasters, sharing nearly equally the schoolrooms, teachers' house and gardens. One was master of the English Department (Grammar, History, Bible, etc.) and the other was head of the Commercial Department (Arithmetic, Geography and Mathematics). The useful arts were also taught, more especially spinning to girls, but this must have been discontinued early this century. The school was yearly examined (generally in July) by the magistrates, councillors and ministers of the town. As the children did not, in accord with the charter, appear in the Town Council Hall, the Council came to them like Mohammed to the mountain of old.

At the examination in 1820, there were present 'no less than 275 boys and girls' and in 1845 the school reached its highest water-mark when the '117th public examination' took place before Sir William Seton, the Provost and Bailies. At that time, Mr Thomas Mackenzie and Mr Archibald Bremner were respectively masters of the Commercial and English Departments.

The Disruption[150] was as heavy a blow to the school as it was to the usefulness of the S.P.C.K., for in 1846 Mr Mackenzie joined the Free Church and had, of course, to leave after 'above 30 years of diligent and successful service'. The result was that Mr Mackenzie was followed by most of his pupils and the High School, or Free Church Institution, was founded. In 1849 the number of pupils was reduced to as low as 150. Mr Bremner held to his post and died in 1866 after close on thirty-five years active work in the school, 'an intelligent and sturdy old Scottish schoolmaster' who had been at college and who, according to an appreciative paragraph in the *Courier*, believed 'in the ancient institution of the tawse'.

Early the next year, Mr Alexander Brownlie, from Fort William School, became Headmaster, when it was contemplated to make the school 'a central training institution for this part of the Highlands'.

---

150 A split in the Established Church in 1843, when 451 ministers left to form the Free Church of Scotland.

Some attempt was made in this direction when the Society's sphere of educational usefulness was further reduced by the Education Act of 1872. Curiously this very idea of a training college is what the Educational Endowments Commission has lately recommended and is likely to be put into practice.

Mr Brownlie left in 1879 and, as the Society was now giving close on twenty Grammar School bursaries, a Secondary Department was added to the school to prepare these bursars for the universities. The present headmaster (Rector, *Invernessicé*)[151] was appointed in the summer of 1880 to carry out this work. The average attendance for last year has been 500 and there are on the roll some 700 pupils.[152]

151 The celebrated Gaelic scholar, Dr Alexander Macbain, who was appointed in 1880 (at the age of 25) and led the school through its most brilliant period of academic scholarship until 1894, when it was transferred to the Burgh.

152 Although the editor possesses no date for this typewritten account, from the comments of John Noble's 'Miscellanea Invernessiana', quoted in the Gaelic Society's article, it would appear that Peter MacGregor's report may have been one of the first original articles written for the *Raining's School Magazine* between the years 1881 and 1884, before he went on to Edinburgh University.

Appendix II

The Military Roads

Wade	Miles	Date
Fort William to Inverness	61	1725–7
		1732–3
Dunkeld to Inverness	102	1728–30
Crieff to Dalnacardoch	43	1730
Dalwhinnie to Fort Augustus	28	1731
Etteridge Cross Road	4	pre-1734

Caulfeild		
Stirling to Crieff	20	1741–2
Dumbarton to Inveraray	44	1744–50
Stirling to Fort William	93	1748–53
Coupar Angus to Fort George	100	1748–57
Tarbet to Crianlarich	16	1752–4
Dalmally to Bonawe	13	1752–4
Fort Augustus to Bernera	43	1755–63
Inveraray to Tyndrum	22	1757–61
*+Stonehaven to Fochabers by Aberdeen	84	1750s
Huntly to Portsoy	20	1750s
°Corgarff to Aberdeen	46	1750s
+Dunkeld to Amulree	9	1761
Contin to Poolewe	52	1761–3
*Fettercairn to Fochabers	66	1761
Bridge of Sark to Port Patrick	105	1760s
Coupar Angus to Dunkeld	15	1760s

Probably Caulfeild, but undated		
Grantown to Aviemore	16	
Sluggan Bridge to Dulnain Bridge	9	
Fort George to Inverness	16	
Grantown to Forres	13	

Post-Caulfeild		
Dulsie Bridge to Aviemore	20	1790s
Fort William to Glencoe	22	1786

Stranraer to Ballantrae	16	1780–2
Dumbarton to Stirling	34	1770–80
Perth to Perth Prison	(960 yd)	1810

*18 miles in common between Huntly and Fochabers
+12 miles in common between Kintore and Aberdeen
°Mileage conjectural

(after Wm Taylor *The Military Roads in Scotland* 1996 by kind permission)

Bibliography

Bede, *A History of the English Church & People* (AD731) trans. by Leo
  Sherley-Price (Penguin Classics 1968)

Boswell, James, *The Journal of a Tour to the Hebrides with Samuel Johnson*
  1785 (Nelson Classics)

Burt, Capt E., *Letters from a Gentleman in the North of Scotland* (Edinburgh,
  1754, 2 vols (repr. 1974)

Cameron, Sir Ewen of Lochiel, *Memoirs* ed. by John Drummond (Edinburgh,
  1842)

Campbell, Dr Duncan, *Reminiscences & Reflections of an Octogenarian
  Highlander* (Northern Counties, 1888, last edn, 1910)

Duncan Millar, Alistair, *A Bit of Breadalbane* (Pentland, 1995)

Fearchair-a-Ghunna: The Ross-shire Wanderer (House of Lochar, 1995)

Ferguson, W., *Scotland 1689 to the Present* (Edinburgh, 1968)

Forbes, Bishop Robert, *Journals of the Episcopal Visitations 1762 & 1770* ed.
  by J. B. Craven (London, 1886)

Fraser, James, *Chronicles of the Frasers: The Wardlaw Manuscript 1674* ed by
  William MacKay 1905 (repr. Scot Hist Soc vol 47 1974)

Fraser, William, *Memorials of the Montgomeries, Earls of Eglinton* (Edinburgh,
  1859)

Gerber, Pat, *The Search for the Stone of Destiny* (Canongate, 1992)

Graham, Henry Gray, *Scottish Men of Letters in the 18th Century* (Black, 1901)

Grant, I. F., *Everyday Life on an Old Highland Farm 1769–1782* (Longmans,
  Green & Co, 1924, new edn pub by Shepherd-Walwyn, 1982)

Grant, Mrs Anne of Laggan, *Letters from the Mountains, 1773–1807* (6th
  edn, 2 vols 1845)

Haldane, A. R. B., *The Drove Roads of Scotland* (Birlinn, 1997)

Hill Burton, J., *Lives of Simon Lord Lovat & Duncan Forbes of Culloden*
  (Chapman & Hall, London, 1847)

Johnson, Samuel, *Journey to the Western Islands* (1775)

Life & Death of Jamie Fleeman, the Laird of Udny's Fool (Aberdeen, 10th edn,
  1810)

MacDonald, Micheil, *The Clans of Scotland* (Trodd, 1991)

MacGregor, Forbes, *Clan Gregor* (The Clan Gregor Soc., 1977)

Mackenzie, Osgood, *100 Years in the Highlands* (1921, new edn, Nat Trust for Scotland with Geoffrey Bles, 1988)

Mackenzie, W.C., *Life of Lovat* (The Moray Press, Edinburgh, 1908)

Mackenzie, W.C., *Lovat of the Forty Five* (Grant & Murray, Edinburgh, 1934)

Mackintosh A.M., *Brigadier Mackintosh of Borlum*

Mackintosh A.M., *The Mackintoshes & Clan Chattan*

Mackintosh of Mackintosh, Sir Eneas, *Notes on Strathdearn* (1774–83)

Macpherson, Alexander, *Church & Social Life in the Highlands* (Blackwood, 1893)

Marshall, *General View of Agriculture in the Central Highlands of Scotland* (1794)

McLaren, Moray, *Lord Lovat of the '45* (Jarrolds, London, 1957)

McLeod, Dr Norman, *Reminiscences of a Highland Parish* (London 1867)

McNeill, F.M., *Iona* (Blackie, 1920, 4th edn, 1954)

McNie, Alan, *Clan Murray* (Cascade, 1988)

New Statistical Accounts of Scotland (1842)

Pennant, Thomas, *A Tour in Scotland & Voyage to the Hebrides* (1790, 3 vols)

Pococke, Bp Richard, *Tours in Scotland 1747, 1750, 1760* (Scottish Historical Society, 1887, 1st Series vol 1)

Prebble, John, *Culloden* (Penguin, 1967)

Ramsay, Dean, *Reminiscences of Scottish Life & Character* (Peter Davies, Edinburgh, 1857, New edn, 1924)

Rennie, James Alan, *Romantic Strathspey, Its Lands, Clans & Legends* (Robert Hale, 1956)

Robertson, James, *Journal* (National Lib of Scotland, 1771 MS2508)

Sinclair, Sir John, *First Statistical Accounts of the Parishes of Scotland* (1791–9, 21 vols)

Sinclair, Sir John, *General View of the Northern Counties & Islands of Scotland* (1795)

Smith née Grant, Elizabeth of Rothiemurchus, *Memoirs of a Highland Lady* (London, 1928)

Stewart, Maj Gen David of Garth, *Sketch of the Manners & Character of the Highlanders in Scotland* (1825)

Swire, Otta F., *Skye: The Island & Its Legends* (Blackie, 1961)

Taylor, William, *The Military Roads in Scotland* (House of Lochar, 1996, 1st edn, 1976)

Places Index

Ordnance Survey Maps (Landranger Series) and Grid References are largely those given by the OS *Gazeteer of Great Britain 1987* pub. by Ordnance Survey & MacMillan Press Ltd – by kind permission.

PLACE NAME[153]	MAP		OS REF	PAGE
Aberdeen/Aberdeenshire	38	–	NJ9206	12, 14, 20–3, 30, 34, 40, 60, 66, 87, 101, 128
Aberfeldy	52	–	NN8549	29
Abernethy	36	–	NH9918	28
Abertarff (dist – see footnote 88)	34	–	NH3708	88, 107
Abriachan	26	–	NH5535	35
Aigas (Is)	26	–	NH4641	88
Aird, The	26	–	NH5642	86, 107, 110
Alvie	35,36	–	NH8609	38–40, 51, 54
Angoulême, France				94
Aonach in Glenmoriston (see footnote 10)	34	–	NH2211	17, 30
Appin (dist)	49	–	NM9950	33
Ardnamurchan (dist)	47,40	–	NM5267	32, 64, 128
Ardvordan (see footnote 50)	36	–		53
Argyll (dist)	50,55,56	–	NN1112	9, 14, 22, 33, 90–102
Arisaig (dist)	40	–	NM6687	110
Armadale	32	–	NG6304	12, 14
Arran (Is)	62,68,69	–	NR9540	14
Arrochar	56	–	NN2904	29
Artrasgart	51	–	NN7247	75
Atholl (dist)	42	–	NN6871	28–29, 85–7, 90–3, 97 99, 105
Auchterblair, Carrbridge	36	–	NH9222	38
Ayr	70	–	NS3422	62
Badenoch (dist)	34,35	–	NN6291	2, 39, 47
Balhaldie	57	–	NN8105	107, 114
Ballachulish	41	–	NN0858	2, 30, 34, 60

---

153 Key: Is = island; dist = district (OS ref represents approximate centre)

Balmerino	54,59	–	NO3524	111
Balnagown	26	–	NH5349	28
Balnain	26	–	NH4430	25
Balnespick	35	–	NH8303	38–55
Banff	29	–	NJ6864	23, 65
Bar-le-Duc, France				95, 96
Beaufort Castle	26	–	NH5043	87, 104, 107, 114
Beauly	26	–	NH5246	3, 22, 69, 107
Beauly Firth	26	–	NH6047	70, 84, 87
Beauly River	26	–	NH5447	84, 88
Beinn Dòrain	50	–	NN3237	26
Belladrum	26	–	NH5241	102
Ben Nevis	41	–	NN1671	111
Black Isle (dist)	21,26,27	–	NH6457	2, 34, 69
Black Mount (dist)	50	–	NN2947	26
Blair Atholl	43	–	NN8765	29
Blantyre, Malawi				37, 121
Boreland	51	–	NN7144	1, 75, 80
Boulogne, France				96
Bourges, France				94
Braemar	43	–	NO1491	28, 34, 97
Breadalbane (dist)	51	–	NN5136	1, 9, 22, 26, 30, 78
Broadford	32	–	NG6423	14
Broughton	72	–	NT1136	109, 111
Bunchrew	26	–	NH6245	87, 97
Burntisland	66	–	NT2386	77
Caithness (dist)	12	–	ND1748	14, 26
Callander	57	–	NN6307	26
Cape Breton (Is), Canada				18
Carolina, USA				17
Carrbridge	36	–	NH9022	1, 2, 29
Castle Leathair (Cas Heather)	26	–	NH6742	96
Castle Menzies	52	–	NN8349	75, 80
Clanranald Estates	40	–	NM6560	19, 32–3
Clett, The	12	–	ND1071	64
Clonard, Co Meath, Eire				120, 122
Clonmacnoise, Co Meath, Eire				130
Clune in Strathdearn	35	–	NH7925	38–9
Cluny	27	–	NJ0753	39–40, 109
Coigach (dist)	15	–	NC1104	32
Coll (Is)	46,47	–	NM1957	14, 22, 32–4
Colonsay (Is)	61	–	NR3794	125, 129

Note: There is considerable variation in convention as to whether glens and straths are named as one word or two. I have tried to follow the nomenclature used by the Ordnance Survey to make it easy to use their Landranger series for identification.

General Index

Note that many of the landowners mentioned in the text were named after the places from which they derived their title. They will therefore be found from the Places Index to save duplication here.